Reinventing Political Culture

Reinventing Political Culture

The Power of Culture versus the Culture of Power

Jeffrey C. Goldfarb

polity

The right of Jeffrey C. Goldfarb to be identified as Author of this Work has been asserted in accordance with the UK Copyright, Designs and Patents Act 1988.

First published in 2012 by Polity Press

Polity Press
65 Bridge Street
Cambridge CB2 1UR, UK

Polity Press
350 Main Street
Malden, MA 02148, USA

ISBN-13: 978-0-7456-4636-7
ISBN-13: 978-0-7456-4637-4(pb)

A catalogue record for this book is available from the British Library.

Typeset in 11 on 13 pt Sabon
by Servis Filmsetting Ltd, Stockport, Cheshire
Printed and bound in Great Britain by the MPG Books Group

The publisher has used its best endeavours to ensure that the URLs for external websites referred to in this book are correct and active at the time of going to press. However, the publisher has no responsibility for the websites and can make no guarantee that a site will remain live or that the content is or will remain appropriate.

Every effort has been made to trace all copyright holders, but if any have been inadvertently overlooked the publisher will be pleased to include any necessary credits in any subsequent reprint or edition.

For further information on Polity, visit our website: www.politybooks.com

Contents

Contents

Introduction

I believe that the reinvention of political culture is critical for addressing pressing problems of our times. I think, further, that reinventing political culture has been a significant ongoing part of political life, even though it has not been recognized as such by political observers, and by scholars of politics and political sociology. I will substantiate my belief and thought by embarking on a theoretically informed journey.

Following this introduction, we will start with a re-examination of the notion of political culture, in a sense, reinventing the concept for the practical tasks at hand. Then, we will explore key sites of reinvention: the terrain around the former Soviet bloc, the American dream and dilemma as represented in the words and deeds of Barack Obama, and the "clash of civilizations" in the Middle East. This will lead us to a synthesis of our comparative investigation, pointing to our conclusions concerning the theoretical problematic of the power of culture versus the culture of power, and considering the classic practical question: "What is to be done?" That is, what is it that we intellectuals should do so that we contribute to the democratic reinvention of political culture?

Reinventing political culture: the concept and the active political project, this is the subject of our inquiry. Before systematically engaging the subject, I will provide an overview by introducing our comparative examples as I first observed them through direct personal experience.

Introduction

The Fall of an Empire

It is one of the good fortunes of my life to have been an eyewitness to the great transformation in the former Soviet bloc. I spent a lot of time doing research in Poland and around the old bloc. I saw the development of zones of autonomous action using official Communist party-state institutions. I observed the development of a democratic opposition, which moved from small independent actions to the development of the great movement of Solidarity. I conspired with the Solidarity underground in minor ways, establishing with one of Poland's leading democratic intellectuals, Adam Michnik, an international clandestine "Democracy Seminar" (Matynia, 1996). I watched with great satisfaction when the natural leaders of society, who had been forced into the shadows, became the real leaders of actually forming democratic polities.[1] And most significantly for the task at hand, I saw how changes in political culture in that part of the world were a key precondition to one of the most fundamental political changes in the modern world.[2] This observation is the starting point of our journey.

The collapse of the old regime is often explained as being sudden, spontaneous, the result of the tough stance Ronald Reagan took in the last stages of the Cold War, or the result of the jihad in Afghanistan. I do not doubt that there were many factors explaining the fundamental geo-political changes, but one that was central and has been generally overlooked is a long transformative cultural march. The changes were not as sudden as is often asserted. People slowly but surely changed the way they related to the official political culture. They changed the stories they told about themselves to themselves, and these stories were intentionally distanced from the official power of the ideological state.

I saw this emerging in the early seventies. I went to Poland, in 1973, to do a comparative study of the organization of theaters in New York and Warsaw. While there, I discovered a zone of independent cultural and political action that was part of a society-wide reinvention of the political culture of socialist Poland. Young and not so young people used the support of the official socialist student organization to create theater groups that were

2

strikingly independent, creating innovative art and a challenging politics, emerging from their own experiences. I realized I was onto something important.

But explaining this to my colleagues and professors was not easy. I remember going into Morris Janowitz's office in September 1974: a nervous young man with a full Jewish afro, looking very much the part of a sixties' radical, meeting the world's leading military sociologist, a hard-nosed political realist.[3] I had just returned from Poland. I was trying to explain to Janowitz, with little success, what I had seen and done, and why my dissertation research on Polish Student Theater was of sociological significance. For me my findings were clear: a theater movement existed in Poland that was strikingly free, and this was changing Polish society in fundamental ways. My task was to develop an adequate explanation for the social support and sociological significance of the independent world they had created. Janowitz just wanted to know: is the movement for or against the regime, Communist or anti-Communist? His was a Cold War question that I could not answer. It was a question embedded within the political common sense of Communism versus anti-Communism. My project, which he never fully accepted, was a post-Communist and post-anti-Communist answer. Although the movement was neither Communist nor anti-Communist, and was not a direct threat to the regime, it also was not apolitical. It did have great political significance. I never quite put it this way then, but it is now clear to me that I was discovering the reinvention of political culture in its early stages.

There was something strikingly different about the theater movement I had studied that it shared with later developments: the democratic opposition in Central Europe in the 1970s and 1980s, and the labor movement, Solidarność both above and underground in the 1980s. Significantly, all developed in the shadow of the events of 1968 in Prague and Warsaw. They were all, in terms of political culture, neither pro- nor anti-Communist. They were beyond that dualism. They destroyed the dualism's descriptive power. While the Central European nations of the former Soviet bloc have become capitalist, committed to liberal democracy and membership in NATO and the EU, the opposition movements in the region, which were the local engines for the transformations of 1989, cannot be explained by these results.

The reinvention of political culture moved from the simple act of ignoring or attempting to subvert official control, to committing to a very different understanding of culture and power. This is beautifully represented in Vaclav Havel's classic essay, "The Power of the Powerless" (Havel, 1985). The first step of this reinvention often was focused on very local concerns: scouting clubs, environmental groups, soccer teams, bread and butter labor unions, theaters such as the ones I studied, and music groups.

An elegant film produced in 1981, *And There Was Jazz*, directed by Feliks Falk, depicts the great significance of those who created, performed, and listened to such work in the 1950s. Because of their participation in the jazz scene in Stalinist Poland, young musicians created an alternative public space for themselves and their audience. Through simple acts of finding instruments, getting together for rehearsals, announcing concerts, and performing, people were able to perform and listen in nearly invisible, very informal locations, beyond the official social order. This added up to be something that was of immediate local significance, for those involved and for those who observed their activities. Because a film was made about such activities, the significance went beyond the local. Society is changed by such phenomena, both the immediate and the mediated. Brought about by specific action, beyond the dominant narratives of the day, such activities add up to a different social order, with a different political culture. From the fictionalized jazz enthusiasts in Falk's film, to the theater I studied, to the great social movement of Solidarity, the secession from official definition and the struggle to redefine the relationship with the powers involved a reinvention of the relationship between power and culture, a fundamental change.

I did not know how to explain this point to Janowitz in his office in 1974. He knew the hard political facts of the Cold War. I saw that his view did not account for the activities where the real action was, that a new zone of autonomous political and cultural activity emerging in Poland was a significant end in itself. Its mere existence changed the nature of Polish society. This was the logic of the movements of transformation that later led up to the historic year 1989. Reinvented political culture, as the power of cultural life confronted the culture of the powers, was a key arena of social change.

Changing Common Sense

In a very different part of the world, in a very different way, the reinvention of political culture has become central to politics and the potential for change in the United States. Particularly noteworthy has been Barack Obama's project to reinvent American political culture by changing political common sense. I, along with many of my fellow citizens, have been deeply moved by Obama. I think that the reasons for this have been too easily dismissed by his opponents, too simply explained by his supporters. He is cool, young, and vibrant. During his campaign for the presidency he revealed a charismatic personality, and gave beautiful speeches. But there was much more to it than that. His eloquence was a response to a social mobilization for greater social justice and the rule of law, against abuses of American power. He spoke profoundly about issues of race and diversity. He promised a change in the relationship between the US and the rest of the world. His quality of mind was revealed in the speeches he had written and delivered, the authenticity of which has been confirmed in his beautifully crafted and insightful books (Obama, 2004, 2006). From a personal point of view, I have been very excited about a political leader who writes better than I do.

The changes that Obama has initiated in American life were not all of his own doing. He stimulated the American imagination, and then had to respond to a changed America, a very interesting interaction which will require careful study throughout his public career. I saw this early on in his national campaign, and as a consequence became part of it.

Like many others, I first became aware of Obama as a national figure when he, as Illinois State Senator, gave his now famous 2004 Democratic National Convention Keynote Address. He inspired a nation by identifying his idiosyncratic personal story, father from Kenya, mother from Kansas, named Barack, with the highest hopes and dreams of America.

> My parents shared not only an improbable love, they shared an abiding faith in the possibilities of this nation. They would give me an African name, Barack, or "blessed," believing that in a tolerant America your name is no barrier to success. They imagined – They imagined me going to the best schools in the land, even though they weren't rich, because in a generous America you don't have to be rich to achieve your potential. (Washington Post, 2004)

I heard about the speech from my son, Sam, who was then living in Obama's neighborhood, Hyde Park, as an undergraduate at the University of Chicago. I was teaching in Kraków, Poland that summer and, in a phone conversation, Sam confidently told my wife, Naomi, and me that we had to listen to the speech, which we had already read about, because Obama would be the next President of the United States (after the winner of the 2004 election). We had our doubts: our common sense and our life experiences told us that an African American President was not on the near horizon, but it turned out that Sam had the wisdom of the young, which repeatedly revealed itself in the years that followed concerning Barack Obama's prospects.

As Obama was elected to the United States Senate, and with talk about his presidential prospects going beyond our family circle, we became early and enthusiastic supporters. He made us believe that there was an alternative, another, better America which he could represent and in which we wanted to be active. We made early modest financial contributions to his campaign, and in turn the campaign identified us, and recruited Naomi in December of 2007 to go to the city of White Plains, New York, near our home, to collect signatures to put Obama's name on the ballot for New York Democratic Primary. She spent an afternoon and collected around twenty signatures. It was hard work. A cold afternoon, people were not yet focused on the election, and those who were did not think that Obama had a chance, nor was he their choice. Remember, Hillary Clinton was our popular Senator. Naomi particularly recalls one African American man who practically laughed in her face that she thought Obama had any chance. Although she did good hard work, I thought I could more easily get as good results at a nearby community center where I swim. And I did.

Our county, Westchester, is residentially segregated. Renowned for wealth, it is actually more diverse economically than its reputation, with significant immigrant neighborhoods and concentrated African American sections, one of which is served by the Theodore Young Community Center. Most of the staff and the patrons of the center are African American, but many other people, Latino, Asian, and white, also use the center, for many different activities. For years, I went to swim. I didn't socialize. I would put in my mile or two, two or three times a week, without making friends and barely having acquaintances. I worked out and went home, that is until I decided to try to match Naomi's collection of signatures, doing so in less than an hour before and after a midday swim.

In a way, it wasn't as easy as I had expected. Many of the staff had their doubts. Before the Primary, Clinton had visited the center as our Senator. As the Primary season opened, Hillary was polling significantly ahead of Obama among African Americans, and if anything at the center this was especially the case. A number of people refused to sign. Most signed right away, particularly when I explained that the issue was getting him on the ballot and not choosing him over Hillary. But they did not think that Obama had a realistic chance and were uncertain about him. To make a long story short, this initiated a series of discussions, activities, and friendships, some of them deep. The community came to support Obama with great passion and I was welcomed as the one who first exhibited that passion when others still had their doubts.

We have followed the campaign and Obama's presidency together, with increasing enthusiasm. I made what became a highly visible bet with a lifeguard, Preston Brown, after he teased me about my believing that Obama would win the Primary campaign. Later, when it was not certain whether Clinton or Obama would prevail in the Democratic contest, we made a second bet. I bet that the Democratic candidate, either Obama or Clinton, would beat McCain. As an experienced black man in his forties, Preston was sure that Americans would vote neither for a black man nor a white woman. Two meals were on the line, which I happily won with a dinner for three, inviting another lifeguard, Tim John, to a lunch at our local Applebees.

As the campaign proceeded, I invited my friends, including Monique Gaston, Pat Richards, Tim Johns, Janet Allen, Ted Dowie, Judith Lee, Norma Jean Barnes, Patricia Roper, and Lee Trollinger, to take part in some campaign activities I was engaged in: a "Barack the Vote" concert on the Hudson River, a phone bank, a trip to campaign in Northwest Philadelphia. They invited me to attend and speak at the community gathering in the gymnasium to watch the inauguration. We all went out for drinks and food to celebrate his victory and again to celebrate his first hundred days.

A particularly key person in this emerging social group was the community center's receptionist, Beverly McCoy. She is vivacious and friendly, knows just about everyone who uses the center, from the young summer campers, to the many senior citizens, from the teenagers taking African dance classes to the elderly Chinese members who meet for Chinese cultural activities. She has just the right word to say to brighten our days ("Happy Tuesday!"). She is the community center's natural community organizer. Obama does not have a stronger supporter than Beverly. If it weren't for Beverly, I would have become a curiosity to the staff and patrons of the center, the white guy who early on was collecting those signatures. Instead I was welcomed into a community.

Around Beverly's reception desk people gather to discuss the problems of the day, a micro-public space to share the fears and concerns about the Tea Party, to discuss the latest news on the health-care debate, to cheer Beverly up when "our guy" is having a hard time, to revel in our success after an accomplishment. These discussions cut across racial and class lines. We openly, or at least more openly than I have ever heard, speak about experiences of racism, intermarriage, inter-racial understandings and misunderstandings, without the recriminations and clichés of the everyday and of abstract theory. Eric Holder, soon after he became Attorney

General, noted in a provocative speech that Americans are cowards when it comes to speaking about race (US Department of Justice, 2009). The exceptional nature of our discussions around Beverly's desk, which my intuition tells me has been repeated in other small American venues since the election of Barack Obama, reveals the truth of Holder's controversial observation. Even in the mass media, with all the stylized performances and cynical manipulations, it seems to me, there has been a change.

Of course, change, as Holder's statement suggest, has its limits, even in our little world. When Preston, Tim, and I had our lunch at Applebees, there was a lot of kidding, a continuation of the exchanges that occurred between us throughout the campaign and which have continued during the Obama presidency. But then especially, Preston needed to underscore that he always wanted Obama to win, just didn't believe that it was possible. He admitted that the victory told him something new about white people, as it told blacks, whites, and other Americans something new about who we are. Yet, the reaction against Obama, the special hatred, the accusations that he is not really an American, the cries for "taking our country back," confirmed that our worst fears are not over and done with, that America is far from being a post-racial society. When it came to paying the check, this sad truth was confirmed in an eerie way. Preston asked for the check and the waiter brought it to me to pay. Two black guys and a white guy. Obviously the white guy would be paying. There was nothing intentionally demeaning in the waiter's gesture. He simply enacted the still prevailing everyday assumptions about race and status in America. The change is that at the community center, we talk about this and that we have connected this talk to the way we act politically. American political culture is being reinvented.

Confronting Them and Us

There is perhaps nowhere in the world where the task of reinvention of political culture is more pressing than in the Middle East, and specifically in Israel–Palestine. The conflict is intractable. It is a classic tragedy, not a confrontation between good and evil, but between two goods, fated to go unrealized, revealing "evil" in the process. A persecuted people, after centuries of oppression and exclusion in Europe, culminating in genocide, find a place for themselves in what they perceive to be their ancient homeland. A peaceful people are forced off their land, displaced, homeless, subjected to second-class citizenship. As Israelis and Palestinians fight against each other in their pursuit of justice, justice is denied. The majority on both sides, at least at times, has even agreed on what they perceive as a just solution, a two-state solution, with Jerusalem as the capital of two nations, but getting there from here has made the solution elusive, if not impossible. Repeated failure has led to despair and aggression. On both sides, majorities are convinced that the other side is not serious about a just resolution, not serious about peace. Against these majorities, some try to keep alternatives alive. Their activities remind me of small things I had observed in the US and in East and Central Europe.

When I first went to Israel, as a Visiting Professor at the Hebrew University in the spring of 2005, I asked people about this resemblance and looked around. I was curious whether my East European and American research on micro-politics, developed in my book *The Politics of Small Things,* which I was then just completing, had application to the situation in Israel and Palestine. I actually had few responsibilities during my stay, two professional lectures, overviews of my book, one in Jerusalem, one in Tel Aviv. I talked to people from around the country about their understanding of the conflict and the alternatives to militarized politics. In the response to my lectures and in my conversations, I heard a wide range of opinions. But there seemed to be a consensus on one point, whether people admired or were critical of the peace movement, whether they approved or disapproved of those who reached across the divides of the conflict, they understood such activities as being of marginal significance. They knew that there were many of these people, but did not think their activities were important. I think they may be mistaken, when the dimension of political culture is kept in mind. As Obama and his fellow Americans are attempting to rewrite American political culture, these people are attempting to reinvent the understanding of the relationship between "them" and "us."

A most compelling example of people who work against the common sense about "the other" is The Parents Circle, a Palestinian Israeli organization of "bereaved families for peace."[4] I first met them at their Israeli headquarters outside of Tel Aviv when a student of mine arranged a meeting. I found it absolutely remarkable how the Israeli and the Palestinian members of the organization worked with each other. I know that when people try to work across divides of conflict and of domination, finding an equal footing is difficult. Condescension and arrogance on the part of the structurally advantaged group members is difficult to avoid, as is acquiescence to subordination or defensive aggression on the part of the members of the dominated group. The warm feeling and the careful avoidance of such pitfalls were striking at the Parents Circle office.

What I saw that day is depicted in *Encounter Point,* a moving film about the group.[5] It introduces ordinary people on both sides of the conflict attempting to re-write the political culture as it accounts for them and us. These are people who have lost loved ones in the conflict: victims of wars, military raids, suicide bombings, terror of the state apparatus, and of resistance organizations. The group members are dedicated to not having their loss used to justify a politics of retribution. It started in Tel Aviv, among a group of Israeli parents. It now has both Palestinian and Israeli branches, with the Palestinian group slightly outnumbering the Israeli one. The groups operate both independently and jointly. Getting together, a crucial part of their endeavors, though, is not easy. Travel restrictions make Palestinian movements within Israel proper difficult, if not impossible. And Israeli citizens also are restricted in their movements in the occupied territories. In the film, we see a group meeting in Jerusalem. What we don't see are the obstacles and checkpoints that had to be surmounted for the Palestinians to take part. We are shown an attempt by the Israeli group to meet a group in the West Bank, and though they finally do get through, their difficulties are clearly depicted. It includes a postscript showing the Palestinian host of the gathering being arrested as a terrorist suspect, but released from prison thanks to his Parents Circle Israeli colleagues. Road blocks, checkpoints, official regulations, and fear are the group's immediate obstacles, but memory and attitudes toward the other are more profound ones.

In the report of the Jerusalem meeting, we see a discussion between two families who lost their daughters to the conflict, in an anti-terrorist military operation in Bethlehem and in a suicide bombing in Tel Aviv. It is a quick empathetic conversation, casual, seemingly not of profound significance. But we see more outside the meeting. We learn that the family from Bethlehem had the bad luck of driving, on a shopping trip, the same model car as a group of suspected terrorists. And when their car came into view of the Israeli army, they were attacked and their daughter was killed. We see the funeral, a full martyr's ceremony, with aggressive nationalist, almost militaristic, rhetoric and with the father actively taking part. And we see the father later, now a member of Parents Circle, as deputy major of the city. This is a moving sequence of events. The family, of course, has not forgotten the loss of their daughter, but in their actions, they are challenging a dominant way of remembering, trying to create another way, apparently with some success.

Their Israeli counterparts do the same thing. We see the father who lost his daughter to the suicide bombing go to school groups and argue not only for peace and reconciliation, but also against the linking of memory and retribution. He may not convince, but he is, at least, opening up new possibilities.

Both fathers know that as they work in their own communities, they make it possible to work together, and in doing so, they are creating new political alternatives to the logic of the central authorities, *by redefining their situation and acting together based on that redefinition.* I am struck by the fact that working against memory, or, at least, "re-remembering," collectively remembering in a different way, is a first act of transforming the common sense about "them and us" and reinventing a political culture.

The two fathers and their fellow members of The Parents Circle meet the other in a different way. Even as they are part of different political communities and may not agree on the big political questions, they share a commitment that their losses should not be used as a key justification for flaming the conflict. Their attempt to de-militarize the conflict suggests a possible overcoming of the tragedy. The obstacles they face are very real. Some, they are able to overcome in their interaction. But the interaction is difficult, requiring changes in fundamental attitudes, but also requiring a subversion of structures that separate people, physical restrictions, and communal attitudes. Nonetheless, these people and many like them persist. There is a prospect for reinventing political culture when we look closely.

I know when these activities are noted in everyday life on both sides of the green line what the most common relatively positive judgment is. Yes, these are nice activities, praiseworthy, but marginal. Here, by reinventing the concept of political culture and making clear that the project of reinventing political culture is of central importance, I will explain why I question this common sense.

Reinvention

Overcoming the tragedy of "them and us" in Israel–Palestine, changing common sense about race in the United States, and contributing to the fall of an empire in East and Central Europe, key instances of the reinvention of political culture, are central to the politics of our day. In Europe, there is now a question mark over whether the Cold War has passed as decisively as first seemed to be the case just a few years ago. In the United States, the fate of the American promise is quite uncertain, fundamentally challenging Americans, and, given the nature of American power, challenging much of the world. And in the Middle East, the whole question of the clash of civilizations is a pressing problem of everyday life, with potential global impact. Does it turn out that behind the ideological façade of the Cold War, there was the raw conflict of great nation states, predicted by Tocqueville to be the clash of the future in *Democracy in America* (2000)? Is the American century

Introduction

to be followed by the decline and fall of American civilization? Are we fated to live with the global consequences of a "clash of civilizations," a zero-sum game centered on the war between terrorists and anti-terrorists? Definitive answers to such questions are elusive. We explore answers with a deliberate consideration of the concept of political culture, to analyze it, and reinvent it (chapter 1), and then to apply this analytic work to central problems of our times, trying to understand these problems, in the former Soviet bloc (chapter 2), the United States (chapter 3), and Israel–Palestine (chapter 4) in a new light. This will lead to theoretical conclusions concerning the forms and relationships between the culture of power and the power of culture (chapter 5) and practical applications to what we intellectuals should do in addressing these and other pressing problems of our times (chapter 6). The first step, to which we now turn, is to clarify the concept of political culture and how more precisely I think its reinvention is a key political problematic.

1

Reinventing the Concept

Alexis de Tocqueville, in his classic *Democracy in America*, demonstrated the importance of political culture. He showed that in order to understand democracy and America, it is necessary to understand the culture that is specific to both, revolving around the cultural orientation of egalitarianism and the social practice of individualism. Later social scientists raised an important issue, more precisely, how does culture make democracy both possible and impossible?[6] They have understood that the grand comparisons that Tocqueville made between aristocracies and democracies need much more specific analysis. They addressed a central issue of our times: what does it take for democracy to appear and solidify? Yet, the answers they came up with worry me. I do not deny that the correlations that they observe are real. Protestant-dominant countries have been more likely to be democratic than Catholic countries in the Americas, as S. Martin Lipset once observed, not to mention Muslim-dominant countries in the rest of the world. I am just not sure exactly what such observations reveal. Democracy has been too unproblematically defined. And culture has been too statically conceived. How different are such findings from the stereotypes of a prevailing common sense? In our times, the worst version: Christians (or worse still Judeo-Christians) are civilized and democratic, while Muslims are barbaric and undemocratic. Yet, we do need to examine how the politics of our times are culturally constituted. This, crucially, includes the way culture supports or undermines voluntary association and democratic

15

participation, as Robert Putnam and his associates have studied, but it also needs to be approached in a more nuanced way.[7] We do need to understand the cultural dimensions of political conflicts, as well as the supports of political consensus, starting with the politics of local interest, including major geo-political conflicts. Thus the project at hand: the reinvention of the concept of political culture drawing upon Tocqueville's great insights, critically appreciating the work of more contemporary social science.

In this chapter, I will show how Tocqueville's study of "democracy in America" illuminates fundamental problems of the analysis of political culture. We will then turn to twentieth-century social science, and more recent studies, to see how the concept was applied to systematic and comparative inquiry in political science and sociology. This will lead us to an examination of what the "political" in political culture is, moving beyond conventional wisdom, trying to rigorously analyze the power in politics, specifically using the sociology of Max Weber and the critical theories of Michel Foucault and Hannah Arendt. We will also consider the problem of the "culture" of political culture, laying the groundwork for a consideration of the relationship between culture and politics as the way political cultures are defined in interaction, the power of culture versus the culture of power, and as the way to comparatively analyze political culture. We start with a review of the concept's development from Tocqueville to modern social science, and proceed with a critique that leads to a reinvention.

Development: Tocqueville

Americans are natural Cartesians, but no one in America reads Descartes. On this ironic note, Alexis de Tocqueville opens the second volume of *Democracy in America,* the first systematic study of political culture, though he did not use the term. Tocqueville's *magnum opus* is a fine guide for understanding what we mean by political culture and a fine starting point for thinking about its reinvention. Tocqueville establishes the primary field of investigation when he describes how the institutions and practices

of democracy, as a form of governance and of association, are correlated with the culture of a democratic society, and he intensively
analyzes this correlation.

Tocqueville's irony reveals his aristocratic ambivalence about
democracy, which informed the subtlety of his analysis. He
bases his study on his contention that equality is a providential
force, a conviction that, though more common now, was not so
common then. He illuminates throughout his classic text how
equality fosters individualism (a neologism which he helped
popularize), for better and for worse. In volume II, chapter 1, "On
the Philosophical Method of the Americans," he maintains that,
cut off as individualists are from an unreflective deference to the
authorities of the past and contemporary authorities, they base
their judgment about what to read upon individual practical calculation. Later this would be called pragmatism, the distinctively
American contribution to the history of philosophy (West, 1989).

Descartes, the world-renowned European philosopher, whose
philosophy demands the questioning of all received authority, a
philosophy based on the critical reasoning of the individual? No
reason to read him because he does not help one get on with practical affairs. This, even though, as Tocqueville maintains, Descartes'
philosophy is the philosophy of a democratic age. Thus, Americans
do not read a philosopher who questions all received philosophic
authority, because they question received authority. They do not
read democratic philosophy because they are, in a sense, democratic philosophers. Tocqueville marvels, admires, and is also
appalled by this situation (for an enactment of this democratic
philosophical approach to a central problem of politics, the question of the public, see the opening chapter of John Dewey's [1991]
The Public and its Problems).

In describing the philosophical approach of Americans,
Tocqueville presents his key insights about political culture,
applied throughout volume 2. He examines how the associations
within a social order shape the attitudes of people, and vice versa,
and he, crucially, understands democracy to be not only a form of
governance, but also a type of human association. More specifically, he explores the culture that supports democracy, the culture

that results from democracy, and the enduring tensions between culture and democracy. His exploration includes the analysis of a variety of complex relationships: religion and autonomous politics, individualism and democratic possibility, equality and freedom, and their social consequences, and egalitarianism and cultural excellence. These have become the standard field of examination in the study of political culture.

Religion is central in the formation of a political culture. In America, Tocqueville maintains, it provides the common commitment that holds Americans together, making for a coherent political community, but doing so in such a way that does not destroy a robust and free political life (2000: 417–24).

In America, individualism sets the grounds for self rule: autonomous political subjects capable of deciding for themselves matters of public and private concern, who are not atomized and engage the interests and needs of their fellow citizens (482–92).

The relationship between the ideals of equality and freedom are central to modern political cultures. Tocqueville thought that in democracies equality is the primary normative ideal, while in aristocracies, freedom is. But he noted that equality without freedom is the grounds for tyranny. He was particularly concerned with the problem of the tyranny of the majority and specifically intrigued by how Americans avoid this tyranny (235–63).

He was fascinated by how democracy, egalitarianism, and individualism transform culture beyond the life of the mind to the full range of human creativity. He was convinced that there is a fundamental tension between equality and cultural excellence. He foresaw a literature, architecture, poetry, and painting of a middling sort. He foresaw mass culture, in which quantity replaces quality, from the making of the apparently fine homes he saw upon arriving in New York harbor, to timepieces, and literature, to theater and the writing of history and the making of monuments (403–78).

And this all suggested a stark tension at the core of democratic society. In the terms of our times, he saw the potential within democracy for mass, and even totalitarian, society. In the graphic words of Tocqueville:

I see an innumerable crowd of like and equal men who revolve on themselves without repose, procuring the small and vulgar pleasures with which they fill their souls. Each of them, withdrawn and apart, is like a stranger to the destiny of all others: his children and his particular friends form the whole human species for him; as for dwelling with his fellow citizens, he is beside them, but does not see them: he touches them but does not feel them; he exists only in himself and himself alone, and if a family still remains for him, one can at least say that he no longer has a native country.

Above these an immense tutelary power is elevated, which alone takes charge of assuring their enjoyments and watching over their fate. It is absolute, detailed, regular, far seeing, and mild. It would resemble paternal power if, like that, it had for its object to prepare men for manhood; but on the contrary, it seeks only to keep them fixed irrevocably in childhood; it likes citizens to enjoy themselves provided that they think only of enjoying themselves. It willingly works for their happiness; but it wants to be the unique agent and sole arbiter of that; it provides for their security, foresees and secures their needs, facilities their pleasures, conducts their principal affairs, directs their industry, regulates their estates, divides their inheritances; can it take away from them entirely the trouble of thinking and the pain of living?

So it is that every day renders the employment of free will less useful and more rare; it confines the action of the will in a smaller space and little by little steals the very use of free will from each citizen. Equality has prepared men for all these things: it has disposed them to tolerate them and often to regard them as a benefit. (663)

Tocqueville did not expect this of America. Americans are not only individualists emanating from their egalitarian situation. They also readily associate, and their free association works against the dangers of the modern tyranny. There is a need to balance individual commitments and an understanding that one's personal situation is linked to the fate of one's fellows. Tocqueville was sanguine that Americans know how to do this, calling it an individualism that is properly understood. But a balance is in order. Too much commitment to individual concerns, separate from commitment to the larger community, and the tyranny Tocqueville imagines is the result. On the other hand, too much commitment to community, especially the community one is born into, that one is part of as a matter of inherited obligation, rather than voluntary commitment, and the dynamism of democratic society is frustrated. Students of political culture view the capacity to voluntarily associate, to turn away from inherited associations and their obligations, and to be individualistic in orientation, all as components of a modern democratic political culture.[8] Tocqueville, rather, sees these things in tension. He does not present a recipe for the culture that will support an enlightened democracy, but a field upon which democracy and its discontents are at play in the democratic age.

A successful political culture for democracy, Tocqueville maintains, is a result of a balance of political and cultural forces. A common cultural core, most often based in religion, what Emile Durkheim would later name a collective conscience (417–24), is necessary to hold a society together. But if this common core, the religious commitment, decides not only theological issues, but political ones as well, there is no room for a free democratic life. Thus Tocqueville asserts that while Christianity provides a strong grounding for democracy, in Islam, there is no democratic potential.

Tocqueville is sometimes wrong about the relationship between culture and democracy, but he is wrong in very interesting ways. This has intriguing implications for our understanding of political culture.

Christianity is a favorable support for the development of democracy first because it fosters equality. The divine equality of souls yields the profane equality of individuals. It further supports democracy because, according to Tocqueville, in contrast to Islam, it recognizes the distinction between the affairs between people and their God, and the affairs among people. Islam cannot support democracy, Tocqueville asserts, as the distinctively modern form of politics, because it does not recognize the distinction between the theological and the political, while Christianity does. There is no doubt ignorance and a Eurocentric prejudice in Tocqueville's political judgments. Islam is barbaric, Christianity civilized, in his prejudiced eyes. But his argument can undo his prejudice. It can be observed that there are many Christians who do not draw the distinctions that Tocqueville understands as being desirable in general, and particularly in the United States, on the issue of abortion for example. And it also can be demonstrated that in the Islamic tradition there are important distinctions that have been made between the laws of God and the laws of man, and the necessity of drawing a clear distinction between the two (Arjomand, 2008). The illumination of the analytic dimensions of political culture and democratic potential can undermine the limitations of Tocqueville's worldview.

When it comes to the issue of the kind of culture that democracies encourage, Tocqueville's personal limitations are again evident, as the power of his analytic framework helps to indicate the way to overcome limitations. As a European and an aristocrat, he did not understand how democracies could support an independent and distinctive culture of quality.

Tocqueville uses a clean logic. Culture, as the arts and sciences, is hierarchical; democracy, egalitarian. The tension between the two yields a culture that appeals to the broad public, that is easily understood without much preparation, that is produced in great quantity, but not specifically concerned with quality. In the cultural work of the United States, and of democracies more generally, we seek to appeal to the broadest popular tastes, compromising quality. Such things are clearly observable.

Yet, Tocqueville misses other things: strikingly, the power of the vernacular. At exactly the time when a literary Renaissance was emerging in America, Emerson, Thoreau, Hawthorne, Melville, et al., Tocqueville judged that fine literature would not be likely in democratic societies. But the works of these authors are reflections upon and reactions to the democratic condition. They are the literary fruits of a democracy. He would not understand how the most theoretical of sciences would flourish under democratic conditions, at institutions of higher education and research in an institutionally differentiated society. He would not expect that English literature would be most vibrant not following aristocratic canons, but as it distanced itself from such canons. In his lifetime, the case in point was the great nineteenth-century American authors, who were at least as excellent as their British colleagues.

This was followed in the twentieth century with the writings of Catha, Fitzgerald, Hemingway, Faulkner, Ellison, Roth, Updike, and Morrison, among many others, and post-colonial writings coming from throughout the former British Empire, Achebe, Rushdie, Sen, et al. The democratic ethos of inclusion of popular sensibilities enriched rather than diminished the literary imagination.

The tension between equality and quality has led not only to mass culture with little literary value, as Tocqueville expected, but to a more open and enriched literature and other arts that have explored the experiences and sensibilities of the previously excluded. The tension he observed between the hierarchy of cultural judgment and the equality of democracy enriched rather than undermined refined cultural pursuits.

Observing these limitations in his judgment underscores the insight of his fundamental framework for considering political culture. It is a field of continuity and contestation, conflict and creativity. Correlations are observed, alternative outcomes can be highlighted, but they do not lead to easy predictions. It is fun to read Tocqueville and consider how he seemed to predict the future of a major superpower, with industrial and post-industrial power, second to none, when industrial capitalism was in its infancy, before the Civil War and the wars of the twentieth century (Reeves, 1982; Lévy, 2007). But his contributions for the study of political culture are more analytical. The analytic insights were developed by social scientists working on the research and theory of modernization.

A Modern Social Scientific Concept

Political culture came to be a major concern in post-World War II social science. The primary issue was straightforward: What are the cultural supports for democracy? Lucian Pye and Sidney Verba worked around a simple formula: economic development + political culture = democracy or dictatorship (1965: 9). Given the presence of an identified set of values, attitudes, and beliefs, democracy is more likely. The social scientific study of political culture wanted to show how specified cultural attitudes support or undermine the establishment and functioning of democratic systems of governance. It specified Tocqueville's analysis for the contemporary situation, at the time of the Cold War, when modernization seemed to have two paths, that of the United States and that of the Soviet Union. The democratic path required, social scientists found in their research, trust beyond immediate primary circles, belief in equality rather than hierarchy, valuing liberty over coercive order, and a commitment to legality. These were among the cultural orientations that analysts of political culture comparatively measured. Pragmatic as opposed to ideological styles of politics, and belief in government output, supported by good experiences with an ongoing political process, and belief in its legitimacy, were also studied. They proposed that such cultural orientations, also already highlighted in Tocqueville, were a necessary cultural basis for democratic life (1965; see also Verba and Nie, 1972; Pye, 1972).

Seymour Martin Lipset put it most bluntly when arguing for the centrality of political culture, as already mentioned above. He bases his argument on broad and clear correlations, "the correlations of democracy with Protestantism and a past British connection point up the importance of cultural factors." He noted that the more Catholic Latin America (including Quebec, which he studied in his comparative study of the United States and Canada) was less democratic; the more Protestant America (including Anglo Canadians) was more democratic (1990: 82). He, further, underscored the negative correlation between Islam and democracy.

What is striking about Lipset's position, which it shares with much of the literature on political culture linked to modernization theory, is that it analyzes both the political and cultural in political culture as they operate within conventionalized institutions. He and they simplify Tocqueville's insights, facilitating empirical inquiry. Democracy and culture are defined by the easily studied institutions of actually existing liberal democracies, i.e., the party and governmental systems, churches, types of voluntary associations (today we would call them NGOs), and so forth.

Although there are real problems with the sorts of generalizations made by these students of political culture, this literature does, nonetheless, contribute to understanding political prospects and their relationship with culture in an important way. It opens to study what is often answered by theoretical assertion. Marxism and liberalism, the dominant theoretical and ideological positions of the late twentieth century, perhaps still dominant, explain the relationship between economics, culture, and politics in opposing but parallel fashion. For Marxism, the relationship between capitalism and democracy is deeply problematic; for liberalism, it is a necessary, if not sufficient, precondition. Work on political culture makes both positions more complex in a fruitful fashion.

Verba, Lipset, and Pye premise their work on notions of modernization and development. They seek to explain how culture matters in these processes. By doing so, they refine a fundamentally liberal position. Economic development alone does not form democracy. They show that culture intervenes. Want to understand why Brazil and Columbia did not develop democracies in the early twentieth century? Study their culture: the economic pre-conditions were there, while the democracy was not. Want to understand whether democracy and human rights will develop in China in the early twenty-first century? Again political culture needs to be considered. Its extraordinary economic development will not be a lone decisive factor. This work addressed geopolitical problems of the Cold War, as it also addresses problems of the twenty-first century.

But there is a thinness in this kind of comparative account of politics and culture, which stands in stark contrast to Tocqueville's approach. The concept of political culture has been too much informed by modernization theory and too often directly linked to the politics of the Cold War. This is very obvious in some cases. But there are more fundamental problems in the way the political and the cultural in political culture are conceptualized that demands the concept's reinvention. Correlations are noted, but how the correlations are sustained is not made clear. Politics is defined operationally, as that which is done in conventional political organizations, institutions, and parties, and culture is defined statically, as an inheritance that predicts political outcomes. It is crucial to move away from the problems of superficial correlation, too easy operationalization, and a static approach in order to reinvent the concept.

Social Capital and Social Interaction

Robert Putnam suggests the direction in which it is necessary to go. Putnam (2000), and others who address the problem of social capital, work to empirically examine how the associational capacity in societies supports and undermines democratic culture and practice. Social relations facilitate the relationship between politics and culture, playing an important role in the making of political culture generally, specifically supporting or undermining democratic political culture.

Putnam is worried about the state of American political culture. His fundamental position, presented in his many books and articles, is that there is a notable decrease in civic activity, what he calls social capital. People in recent years are less likely to take part in voluntary associations and as a consequence they are also less likely to take part in political life, challenging the legitimacy and vitality of American democracy. The decrease in civic activity affects life chances, social mobility, and economic output, along with the quality of political institutions. Because they bowl alone, literally and metaphorically speaking, Americans vote less and are less politically active and contribute less effectively to their own private advancement and to the common good. His most basic empirical observation, as he put it in his classic essay, "Bowling Alone" (1995) – "Recently, American social scientists of a neo-Tocquevillean bent have unearthed a wide range of empirical evidence that the quality of public life and the performance of social institutions (and not only in America) are indeed powerfully influenced by norms and networks of civic engagement." He observes a long-term trend, the rise and fall of civic engagement, posits a generational and media explanation for the trend (1996), and identifies a social and political crisis.

Putnam clearly sees himself as a neo-Tocquevillian, documenting the link between association and a healthy democracy. He analyzes the reasons for the decline of association, the contrasting qualities of different sorts of association, and the consequences of the decline in quality and quantity. Like earlier students of political culture, he understands that culture matters (a particular concern of his is trust), but unlike them, he embeds the relationship between culture and power within patterns of association, from which, he posits, democratic attitudes come. The values of democracy, both those that arise as a consequence of democratic life and those that support democratic life, are seen to be supported through civic association. Society is the intervening variable between politics and culture.

The "bowling alone" thesis has generated a large literature, applying and criticizing his framework. On the one hand, the long-term trend is questioned. Are people now really bowling alone, or, less melodramatically, are there really fewer consequential civic associations? What are the causes of the changes? And how significant have the changes been? On the other hand, is the connection between civic association and politics really of the sort that Putnam imagines? Might there not be important factors that make it so that some associations are more politically consequential than others? Much of the criticism and debate has addressed the first set of questions, but more interesting, in my judgment, is the second set.

There is the contention that there is no decline. While people may be bowling alone these days, they are actually joining large groups. Instead of the local PTA, the Parent Teachers Associations, there is NOW, the National Organization of Women, for example. But then there is the question of whether such large groups instill the degree of attachment and the cultivation of cultural commitments that more face-to-face organizations do. It may be that the NOW is even more politically important than the PTA has ever been, but the associations in the latter form may be more important than the associations of the former in the cultivation of "the habits of the heart," as Tocqueville named the moral and ethical supports of politics. Judging such matters is a question of political as well as theoretical judgment, the relative importance of the cultivation of active support of traditional community life versus the cultural and political support of feminism, in our example. There is a conservative–liberal political discussion going on here.

Avoiding the political debate, through sociological research, Gary Alan Fine and his colleagues shift our attention to the study of the internal dynamics of small groups, what they call "microfoundations of civic society" (Fine and Harrington, 2004).[9] Their fundamental argument is that small groups are the social forms where civic engagement is enacted and where the results of civic engagement can be observed and studied. As Fine and Harrington put it:

> Ultimately, small groups constitute a behavioral and discursive space in which civil society is created and enacted. We propose three broad roles for small groups in the civic arena. First, groups are the crucible in which civil society is created. Groups define the terms of civic engagement, provide essential resources – such as networks of participants and the construction of identity – and link movements to larger political and cultural themes. Second, small groups provide a space for the enactment of civic engagement by serving as a vehicle for the distribution and maintenance of collective goods. Finally, small groups are an outcome of civic engagement, with participation and proliferation of groups contributing to social and political health. (2004: 344)

In this quote and in much of his work, Fine is highlighting the importance of small groups, how they are constituted, and what goes on within them, for the investigation of not only small but also large sociological problems. He moves us away from global generalizations towards close analysis.

Fine notes that just about no one bowls alone. They bowl in groups that are formally interconnected in leagues and in groups that do not have such explicit ties. And he shows why it is that the degree of formality may not be the crucial factor in determining political and cultural outcomes. What actually goes on in groups and how they connect with others may be much more important.

The internal life of the groups themselves, then, and not just the category of groupings, needs close examination. Thus, PTAs may provide reasons for not engaging in broader civic and political life. They may foster atomization as well as become the basis of broader political connection. And organizations such as NOW, even though membership does not demand much commitment, may in social groups push the members to engage in public issues both locally and more broadly. This is something that must be investigated. Some association is clearly necessary, as in Putnam's key proposition, but the kinds of associations that support and undermine a vibrant democracy may be quite different than he assumes.

If the main thrust of Lipset and Pye is that culture matters and the main contribution of Putnam is that society matters, Fine points us in the direction of paying attention to the details of everyday life, not just macro indicators, but the specificity of human interactions in groups. Nina Eliasoph builds on this theoretical development (1998). She critically examines the specific links between association and political engagement. By looking more closely at what people actually think and do in groups, she questions Putnam's and, by implication, Tocqueville's generalizations. The connection between small group associations and politics, both local and political, is interactively constituted. An etiquette is constituted which may or may not connect self-interest and political concern, forging a connection or breaking it. This is shaped by pre-existing beliefs (what she calls inner sources), and larger structural factors, class relations, the power of the state, etc. (what she calls outer sources), but she demonstrates through careful ethnography how people develop among themselves practices of engaging or not engaging broader public concerns in their group life. She confirms the major assertion in my book *The Politics of Small Things*: democracy is in the details. Here an engaged democratic culture is constituted in the details of associational life.

Studying recreational, volunteer, and activist associations, Eliasoph sees a major problem in the political culture of association in the United States: "The problem comes when people *always* emphasize selfish motives and *always* muffle analysis; when the effort to be unpretentious and inclusive actually *hides* citizens' public-spiritedness . . ." (245). As a student of Robert Bellah, she is concerned that Americans explain their understanding of their civic engagements in the language of individualism and selfishness (Bellah et al., 1985), but she takes this a step further, noting how, while they can and do tap more public ideals in private conversation, they were reluctant to do so in public. Ironically they reveal their selfishness and conceal their higher ideals in public, with the partial exception of their religion. A democratic political culture, in Eliasoph's account, is one where the connections are more readily made.

The sociological move of Putnam, Fine, and Eliasoph, among others (see especially Eliasoph and Lichterman, 2003; Lichterman, 1996; Schudson, 1989a, 1989b), is an important one. By considering human beings in their associations, and especially by examining them interacting culturally and politically in the associations, the workings of political culture can more readily by observed, appraised, and indeed reinvented. Yet, this sociological move, like the work of the mid-century researchers of political culture, leaves unexamined what the politics and the culture of political culture are. There is an understanding that civil society and the public matter for political culture, something I will explore more fully in chapter 5, but missing is a rigorous analytic account of politics and culture and their relationship. This move is key to advancing critical comparative inquiry.

Critique: The Power in the Political

Although much of political life is found in political parties, governmental institutions, and other explicitly political organizations, a great deal of political action occurs beyond these settings. Recall my exchange with Morris Janowitz reported in the introduction. His realistic approach to politics overlooked the political outside of established political institutions. He could not understand the political nature of social action that did not directly engage, either for or against, established political institutions, either Communist or anti-Communist. Such an approach could not apprehend the great political changes that were emerging in East Central Europe. It could not account for the political power that was emerging beyond official institutions. But when the political is not defined operationally, its definition becomes unclear. There needs to be a special effort to precisely understand the political as a sociological form, specifically the sociology of the power of politics. Consider an implicit debate about power among three master thinkers of the twentieth century.

Max Weber tells us that the power of politics, centrally, is a matter of coercion. Power is the ability of one person, "*A*," to get another person, "*B*," to do what *A* wants independent of *B*'s will. *A* could get the job done with physical coercion, say a gun, but more common is that the power is justified, viewed by *B* as being legitimate for one of a variety of different reasons. A command could be accepted because it follows a tradition, is inspired by a charismatic figure, or appraised as being rational and legal, i.e., Weber's ideal type of authority (legitimated power): traditional, charismatic, and bureaucratic (1978: 217).

Hannah Arendt directly opposes this position. Political power is the opposite of coercion. This power is not something that is enforced but collaboratively created. People meet each other, talk, and act in each other's presence and develop a capacity to act in concert. It is that capacity that is the power of politics (1961: 237).

Michel Foucault's position is less clear, but of great importance. He depicts power that occurs behind peoples' backs, beyond coercion and concerted action, as a truth regime, where knowledge and power are two sides of the same coin. He is interested in exactly our problem, how power is not only a part of explicitly political bodies, specifically the state, but rather is something that permeates the social order. He works to reorient political theory. As he graphically puts it: "What we need is a political philosophy that isn't erected around the problem of sovereignty, nor therefore, around the problems of law and prohibition. We need to cut off the king's head: in political theory that has still to be done" (1984: 63). Foucault highlights the importance of power enacted in all the nooks and crannies of social life: in prisons and schools, or in sexual relations, not only, or even primarily, in political institutions.

These are not three competing theories about the same thing, but rather three examinations of power, which are related but need to be distinguished, as we examine the relationship between politics and culture. They illuminate pressing problems of political culture as they highlight the complexities of the political side of the issue.

In the previously existing socialist order of the Soviet bloc, an odd form of the Weberian power was evident. It was hard to find anyone who actually subscribed to the official ideology, who believed the story it told about history and the role of the party-state. Yet the system persisted in the post-Stalinist era without terror and brutal policing, and less repression than, for example, was evident in contemporary Latin American dictatorships, but also without popular support. Despite the absence of social commitment to the system and with only a relatively low-level repression, the then prevailing political order persisted for many years. People interacted as if they believed in the system, and through such action the system persisted. It did not matter what people privately believed, if they oriented their lives and acted guided by the official account of social life, the power of official-dom was confirmed.[10]

Understanding this, two of the leading critical intellectuals proposed a simple course of action, in Vaclav Havel's words "living in truth," or as Adam Michnik put it, to act together as if you lived in a free society (1987; Havel, 1985). They understood that when people respond to the authorities as if they were legitimate, the official authority was confirmed. And if they no longer so acted, the system would be fundamentally challenged. Their common political project was to embark on this challenge. But the apparent simplicity of such reorientation, such a challenge to power, is actually much more difficult than it appears, as we will see in chapter 2. It involves not only saying no to the culture of power, but also creating a new culture to sustain a new power. The challenge to the legitimacy of the authorities was key. In the process of the challenge a truth regime was deconstructed and new ways of acting in concert were constituted, i.e., the three approaches to power were and are closely connected.

The sort of power Arendt highlighted played a key role in the history of the struggle for racial justice in the United States. The civil rights movement was about the poor and the institutionally powerless developing an alternative power. People met each other, spoke, and acted as individuals in each other's presence, and acted in concert: in the churches of such leaders as Martin Luther King Jr., but also in traditionally African American colleges and universities, and in and through the black press.[11] They developed strategies to sustain their individual and collective dignity, and among themselves this was immediately achieved, from the Niagara Movement to the NAACP to the black power movements of the 1960s. They challenged the racist norms of American society, and succeeded on many fronts. There is power in these actions, the sort Arendt highlighted. It may not be the case that political power *is* the opposite of coercion, as she maintained. But she certainly reveals a kind of power, a kind of power that has been central to American politics and culture, as we will examine closely in chapter 3. We will see that coming together, speaking to each other, and acting in concert is harder than it would seem. The rhetoric of legitimate authority must be challenged. A kind of truth regime, the regime of common sense has to be transformed. It requires cultural grounds upon which to meet, and this is far from an easy matter.

Such common ground is elusive in the Middle East, and in many ways seems to be beside the point. As Israeli Jews and Palestinian Muslims and Christians confront each other in Israel, the West Bank, and Gaza, the power of military force and coercion are very much present and seem to define the situation, a sovereign state and its army versus armed resistance. But perhaps more decisive in the ongoing tragedy is the power dynamics of knowledge and power in Foucault's sense. Israel demands that it be recognized as a Jewish state. This is a precondition for talks with Palestinian authorities and a Foreign Minister of Israel, Avigdor Lieberman, has even wanted to make it a requirement for Palestinians with Israeli citizenship, "Israeli Arabs," to maintain their citizenship (see Khoury and Ravid, 2010). On the other hand, the strongest opponents of the Jewish state refuse to call it Israel, but rather refer to the Zionist entity. There is the Israeli war of Independence and *al Nakbha*, the catastrophe. There is the Israeli presence in Judea and Samaria, versus the occupation of the West Bank, the Wall versus the Separation Fence. Among Palestinians, resistance often is equated with armed struggle. "The right of return" is a fundamental condition of Palestinian dignity on the one hand, and on the other, it assures the termination of the Jewish state. Two, radically opposed, ways of knowing empower the two sides of the conflict. The incompatibility of the truths associated with the ways of knowing defines tragedy. Even the archaeological record is sifted and judged in such a way that one side's key artifacts are discarded by the other side, and pointing this out is understood as a major ideological attack, not worthy of academic recognition (Abu El-Haj, 2002). Knowledge and power are intimately connected. From a Foucaultian theoretical position, the power and culture of political culture are identified.[12] But there is room for concerted action that undermines this. There are struggles for alternative ways of justifying action both on the center stage of the political arena and on its margins, as we will observe in chapter 5.

These three ways of considering political power illuminate the relationships between politics and culture, how politics affects and is affected by culture, making up political culture. How authority is legitimated, how people come together, how knowledge empowers: these are the power dimensions of political culture. We will explore this below in each of our comparative cases. Informing that exploration requires, also, a clearer analytic understanding of culture.

Critique: Culture as Destiny and as Creativity

I agree fundamentally with Clifford Geertz on the meaning of culture. He wants to make it clear that it is not as elusive a concept as is often purported. "The culture concept to which I adhere [Geertz writes] has neither multiple referents nor, so far as I can see, any unusual ambiguity: it denotes an historically transmitted pattern of meanings embodied in symbols, a system of inherited conceptions expressed in symbolic forms by means of which men communicate, perpetuate, and develop their knowledge about and attitudes toward life. Of course, terms such as "meaning," "symbol," and "conception" cry out for explication" (1977: 89). And meaning, symbol, and conception, I would add, are the cultural material of political culture, best understood in concrete examples, such as the ones we have and will examine. This conception of culture is one that is implicit in Tocqueville and quite explicit among the social scientists and political observers who use the concept of political culture.

Yet, there is a problem. Culture is a domain both of inheritance and transformation. When culture is a subject of inquiry apart from politics, in the study of the arts and sciences, its creative dimension is commonly given close attention (Goldfarb, 2005). But oddly, when culture is used in political analysis, it is considered primarily as an inherited body of knowledge and orientation that serves to delimit rather than open fields of action. Culture too often is used to explain political fate. There needs to be a special effort to precisely understand the culture in political culture as a sociological form that not only involves inheritance but also creativity and critique. The creative dimension of culture needs to be related to the power dimensions of politics.

This is best approached, in my judgment, within the tradition of Max Weber and the critical theory of the Frankfurt school. Although Weber's sociology is centered on a highly generalized understanding of culture, from which Geertz developed his approach, he also opened the way for a more specific, critical approach. "Art," Weber asserted, is "a cosmos of more and more consciously grasped independent values which exist in their own right [taking on] the function of this-worldly salvation" (Gerth and Mills, 1958). This, position, first outlined as a sociological problem in "Religious Rejections of the World," an exploration of zones of meaning in modernity, was a basic element of the Frankfurt School critiques of the culture industry and affirmative culture (Horkheimer and Adorno, 2007; Marcuse, 1964). What

Weber and Adorno et al. appreciated is that culture, as the arts and sciences broadly understood, has an importance independent of the developments of capitalism and the modern state and the logic of their administration. The arts, philosophy, and the sciences present critical alternatives to the dominant value system, and its meanings, which Weber observed and the members of the Frankfurt School feared was disappearing under the conditions of advanced capitalism. I believe that this notion of culture, along with the notion of Geertz, the two Weberian accounts, dynamically contribute to the constitution and reinvention of political culture. This has been my approach.

I started with a study of alternative theater in Poland (Goldfarb, 1980). I showed how a cultural form persisted despite systematic constraints, justified by the official ideology, and analyzed the contest between the persistence and the constraints, and considered how the cultural work provided a critical understanding of socialist Poland and the possibility of alternatives beyond the theater domain. This led to a comparative structural analysis of cultural freedom (Goldfarb, 1983). I explored public life in Poland and America as cultural life was sustained by the independent ideals of relatively autonomous cultural life. Cultural freedom is sociologically constituted by sustaining an ongoing and free conversation through time and space in the "language" of a cultural form. This conversation develops apart from the logic of the reproduction of the chief steering mechanism of the social order, whether of the market or of the party-state. These early studies were focused on the critical side of things, how critical values and creative accomplishments persisted despite constraints.

In my later works, I shifted from an emphasis on the problem of the persistence of independent cultural creation to the struggle over meaning, informed by not only the powers, but independent creative culture in the former Soviet bloc (Goldfarb, 1989) and in the United States (Goldfarb, 1991). Both these studies utilized free cultural works to develop a critical stance towards the dominant practices of politics. In retrospect, in light of our inquiry, these were studies of how such independent cultural works contribute to the reinvention of political culture. In *Beyond Glasnost,* I showed how the accomplishments of a critical culture formed an independent stance that went beyond the language of newspeak, beyond official ideology, and opened up the possibility of an alternative democratic politics; something that became a reality, months after the publication of the book. In *The Cynical Society,* I used the sensibility of the Central European oppositional democratic culture, to do a critique of my own society. American independent cultural traditions, as they are institutionalized in our social institutions, make it possible to avoid political enervation, make it possible for Americans to realize the possibility of critical action, the political opposite of the cynicism that prevails in much of political life and the media portrayal of that life.

In the context of the end of the Cold War, I then embarked upon investigations of the transition to democracy in Central Europe (Goldfarb, 1992) and the problem of the role of intellectuals in democratic societies (Goldfarb, 1998). In each of these studies, the tension between the practice of an autonomous culture and other social practices provided insight into central historical developments. Intellectuals have been responsible for some of the worst horrors of the twentieth century. In *After the Fall,* I presented an overview of those who were trying to do the opposite on the European killing fields. In *Civility and Subversion,* I specified the democratic role of the intellectual, to provoke talk, to develop informed discussion about the problems faced by a society. When intellectuals do more, when they provide definitive answers, they do worse, they undermine democratic capacity.

In the chapters that follow, I will utilize this approach to culture, a double-edged Weberian one, developed in these previous studies at it relates to the problem at hand, the study of the reinvention of political culture. I will be making explicit what was implicit in my previous work. But before proceeding to this, I want to make clear, through an overview of the cases at hand, the reason for this dualistic Weberian approach. The culture in political culture is not only about inheritance of systems of meaning, but also about creative transformation of such systems.

Poles have often been viewed by their neighbors, and the people of Poland have often viewed themselves, as romantics, more concerned with honor than with practicality, willing to make grand gestures in defense of the nation, instead of calculating national interests realistically. Czechs, on the other hand, have been viewed as realists, knowing all too well when to compromise, when to surrender. These everyday accounts about Polish and Czech political culture are very much a part of the political reality. The persistence of resistance in Poland and the failure to achieve an independent nation state in the nineteenth century, and the instability of the Polish nation state in the twentieth , account for the Polish stereotype. The accommodation of the Czechs to larger forces beyond their control, the Habsburgs, the Nazis, the Communists, suggest the origins of the Czech stereotype.

But these common-sense accounts of political culture conceal as well as reveal. In the last decades of the previously existing socialism of the Soviet bloc, in both places, a common strategy of resistance developed. The accommodating Czechs lived in truth, as their opposition leader Vaclav Havel imagined they might. They developed the Charter movement (named after their oppositional manifesto Charter 77) which led to their famous, creative, even romantic "Velvet Revolution," the first of the now globalized colored revolutions. And the impractical Poles developed the "self-limiting" revolution of Solidarity, grounded in practical actions of sustaining an independent labor movement concerned with everyday issues of social welfare, existing as an underground movement dedicated to the exchange of alternative views rather than the challenging of the political order. Indeed, when the chance came to take control of the political order, the leaders of the movement were notably unprepared. Their practical realism did not foresee a revolutionary shift. My point is not that the common-sense descriptions of political culture are necessarily wrong, but that they are too static. The romantic Poles creatively used their cultural resources and transformed their political culture in a very realistic direction. The realistic Czechs creatively used their resources and moved their political culture in a heroic direction.

In the United States also, political culture has been transformed, from a nation where racism was a primary marker, to one where anti-racism may be more definitive. Anti-racism has a long and distinguished history in the United States, as old as the republic itself. But for the first time in American history, this tradition is officially dominant, with Barack Obama as President. Overcoming a tradition of racism is a great challenge, and it has not been fully accomplished with the election of Obama, just as civil rights demonstrations and the passing of civil rights legislation and key decisions by the Supreme Court did not change the situation completely. But the political culture has been changed.

It is very difficult to imagine such a change in Israel–Palestine, where the definition of one nation seems to be predicated upon the disappearance of the other. For Jewish Israelis, their country must be understood and recognized as the Jewish homeland, the historical land of the Jews, the answer to the long history of anti-Semitism in the Diaspora. This has led to an insistence upon the definition of Israel as the Jewish state, a position which is at odds with the fact that twenty percent of Israel's population is made up of Palestinian Muslims and Christians (not including the occupied territories). They are purported to have equal citizenship, but in fact by definition and by policy practice, they do not. And beyond Israel proper, in the occupied territories, the demographic facts are even more inconvenient. On the other hand, for Palestinians inside Israel, in the towns and villages of the West Bank and Gaza, and in exile in surrounding nations and beyond, in and outside of refugee camps, the right of return, the right of the displaced to return to their homes, is a fundamental commitment. Given the natural population expansion and the development of the land since 1948, this would effectively end the state of Israel.

These two positions, the Jewish state and the right of return, which clearly involve viable notions of social and political justice, are incompatible. Yet, both positions have evolved over time. There was a time, during the British mandate, that a bi-national state was a matter of principle for some Zionists, most prominently the intellectuals around Brit Shalom. It now has become the starting point for some secular radicals, while a two-state solution is generally agreed upon by realists and majorities on both sides of the conflict. A group of independent leaders and activists, Palestinians and Israelis, in the Geneva Agreements, have even negotiated the general contours of a complete settlement along these lines. This solution includes creatively interpreting fundamental principles so that they can become compatible. Particularly interesting, as mentioned in the introduction, and as we will explore more systematically in chapter 5, is how people on the ground act upon such creative interpretations of fundamental principles to get on with their specific projects. Their situated mutual cultural understanding may not directly address the problem of state power and its legitimation, but it does provide the grounds for concerted action beyond the conflict, and situationally uncouples the link between power and knowledge as Foucault would understand it. It is in such a way that struggles over the recreation of political culture are developed.

The Culture of Power versus the Power of Culture

Political culture – can't live with it, can't live without it. This is my general appraisal of the concept of political culture. As the concept was developed in post-World War II social science, it was too tied to the theory of modernization and to the politics of the Cold War. But the concept's central focus, that there is a crucial cultural dimension to politics, as first revealed in Tocqueville's work, is, nonetheless, compelling, explaining why the notion persists. The central point: in order to understand the political world, we must understand how culture facilitates and undermines politics, and how politics shapes culture. My key theoretical proposition: in order to do this successfully, we must understand more precisely what the culture and the political in political culture are. We proceed with the understanding that the political of political culture is based on different dimensions of power, the power of coercion and its legitimation, the power of concerted action, and the power of the truth regime, and that culture is not only a matter of destiny, but also of creativity. We will examine the relationships between power and culture as they persist and are changed in specific settings. I will demonstrate the theory as we use the notion of the reinvention of political culture to understand central problems of our times.

On the relationships between power and culture: we will observe that these are variable, dynamic, definitive. I will show that the issue is not only about the substance of the relationship, but also its degree of intimacy, how closely or distanced power and culture are related. It is significant that Israel is defined by the notion of being a Jewish state, that the American conception of political freedom is constructed as the opposite of being enslaved (Paterson, 1985), and that in previously existing socialism the workers of the world were said to be uniting. Such notions formed a cultural basis of power. They legitimated authority. They provided grounds for common action. They empowered the order of things. They are the different faces of the culture of power. But crucial differences exist in the political orders of the previously existing socialist orders in the former Soviet bloc, of the United States today as opposed to in the past, and of Palestine and Israel, having to do with how closely power and culture have been linked.

Foucault emphasizes that truth and power are two sides of the same coin. My point here is that sometimes and in some places this is truer than at other times and other places. Sometimes, power and culture are linked officially, as in the United States when racism was built into the constitution and in Supreme Court decision making. This was even more clearly the case in the former Soviet bloc, where a political elite ruled using an official ideology, using the power of the party-state apparatus to enforce an official truth. When racism was no longer a matter of public policy and knowledge in the United States, and when the party's truth was no longer the only truth permitted in public interaction in the former Soviet bloc, there were major transformations. In the following chapters, we will examine the struggle for such reinvention, based upon the power of an independent culture against the culture of power.

2

Ideology Ends Again? Around the Soviet Bloc and Beyond

Marxism was alive and well before 1989, despite the proclamations to the contrary in the late 1950s and early 1960s, when ideology was purported to have ended (Bell, 1960). Before the fall of the Berlin Wall, it seemed that there were two different paths to modernity,[13] the socialist and the capitalist, and Marxism flourished both as an ideological account of the accomplishments of the former and a critical tool to appraise the problems of the latter. Marxism was an important part of the political culture of those times, mostly in ways that have been clear. Official Marxism in the Soviet bloc was used to justify the then existing socialism, and sometimes was used by internal critics. And in the West, a rich variety of Marxisms, in competition, were used to develop critical theories and historical analyses in the academy and beyond, and to support and justify a wide variety of political and social movements and parties.[14]

Yet, there is one crucial way that Marxism lived in political culture then that has not generally been understood. Marxism was a key part of the everyday life of previously existing socialist societies. In this chapter, we will explore how this part of the history of the theory contributed to the political culture of those times, and how this part of the history of Marxism contributed as well to the reinvention of political culture. I will present an analysis of how the dynamics of ideology in the political culture of everyday experience played a significant role in the Cold War political order, in the breakdown of the Cold War, and in the constitution

41

of the politics and culture of our times. The problem of ideology, then and now, will be examined. The possibility of politics in a post-ideological age will be considered along with evidence of the development of new ideological forces, to be investigated more fully in the chapters following this one.

Ideology and Power

The notion of ideology is intimately connected to the history of Marxism and the politics of everyday life in previously existing socialism. Karl Marx, along with Frederick Engels, originally used the term in their book *The German Ideology*. Their fundamental position is summarized in a simple proposition: "The ruling ideas of the time are the ideas of the ruling class." With this proposition in mind, Marx and Engels dismissed the ideas of the idealistic young Hegelians. Theirs was an ideology, a false philosophy, justifying the class order as they found it, or at least not disrupting it. Distinct from such idealism, was historical materialism, the philosophy of the working class, the universally exploited class, which yielded truth rather than delusion. In Marx's hands, ideology is contrasted with the truth. This idea of ideology informed existing socialist cultural policy. There were bourgeois social science and scientific historical materialism, the former ideological, the latter the means to truth, and even in biology, there was the dialectical materialist position on the evolutionary development, the infamous position of Lysenko and his colleagues, and there was the reactionary ideology of genetics (Joravsky, 1986). For many years, genetics and sociology were not only labeled as being ideology. They were forbidden.

Vladimir Lenin (1905) in a seminal article on the party press developed a different, politically consequential, position. In arguing for the censorship of the party press, and the consistency of its viewpoint, he called for a party propaganda and ideology. The bourgeois press had bourgeois ideology. The party press should be informed by working class, party ideology. Official practice based on Lenin's early position led to the professional position of "The

Party Ideologist" and important bureaus developing and propagating ideology. This turn suggested not the contrast between ideology and truth, as developed by Marx; rather, there was the battle of ideologies. The battle led to a distinct institutional formation of education, media, the arts, and the sciences, and the attachment of ideological officials to just about all social institutions, from universities to the military. In a wide variety of social locations one battled the class enemy with party ideology. Even on buildings and road signs, in the place of commercial advertising ubiquitous in the capitalist world, there were the equally ubiquitous party slogans. There were the old favorites, from "workers of the world unite," to the almost consumerist "more and more, better and better," (the latter was everywhere to be seen in Poland when I lived there in the early 1970s).

The position of Marx and the position of Lenin, ideology as contrasted to truth and ideology as a weapon of class conflict, were built into the previously existing socialist system. They were definitive of a specific political culture, of a distinctive set of relationships between power and culture. There were a unique truth regime and a specific form of legitimation of authority, and grounds for social mobilization.

a. *Truth Regime:* Foucault tells us that there is no distinction between truth and power, that they are two sides of the same coin. Although I doubt that this is generally true, it was the case in the previously existing socialist order, summarized by the fact that there was an official truth. Not only did this apply to the cases of sociology and genetics, as already mentioned. It included just about every aspect of social life. Atheism, collective farms, grand industrial steel works, and the like were mandated by the truth of Marxism, and the power of the party confirmed truth. Because "religion is the opiate of the people," as Marx declared, party policy systematically undermined religious institutions and belief. Because of the scientific validity of the Marxist critique of the political economy of capitalism, private farms were destroyed and collective farms formed. And when in the Soviet Ukraine moderately successful private farmers resisted, they were identified as class enemies, "kulaks," and defeated, leading to mass starvation and a systemically weak agricultural system (Conquest, 1986). The theory indicated that collectivization defined progress. The party-state enforced it. Empirical consequences and mass human suffering were ignored. Indeed economic planning as a whole was not only concerned with performance, but as much with validation of scientific Marxism. Grand industrial steel works, such as those of Nowa Huta in Poland outside of Kraków, were as much monuments to socialism, in this case standing as a contrast to the traditionalist city down the block, as they were part of a rational economic plan. More precisely, the theory revealed how the monument and plan worked together.

b. *Legitimation of Authority:* Weber explained how power is amplified by its various forms of legitimation: charismatic, traditional, and rational legal. There are kinds of legitimation that he did not recognize. Strikingly, he did not really examine how power is legitimated through deliberation and agreement, even if not consensus. This is a serious omission. Weber did not really understand the possibilities of democratic governance. That he did not foresee ideological legitimation, on the other hand, is primarily because it had not yet fully appeared. Something new and different developed in the twentieth century, commonly identified as totalitarianism. A unique combination of terror and ideology distinguished modern tyranny from its historic predecessors, as Hannah Arendt concluded in her classic study *The Origins of Totalitarianism* (1968). The totalitarian uses terror to instill fear. Not only the guilty, but also the innocent are vulnerable, enforcing atomization and through it domination. Ideology, on the other hand, provides the language of governance and compliance. It provides the script that accounts for the rule. It is the language of power, which has an officially enforced account of the past, present, and future, where the future, as Arendt ironically noted, is most certain. Eggs had to be cracked, as the old Stalinist quip put it, to cook the socialist omelet; even immediate suffering observed in the present would have to be endured for the building of socialism, or of the Third Reich for that matter. The ideology inserted the language of the ruling regime into everyday practices, making it so that these practices could not be achieved without recourse to the prevailing political order. When Havel tells his famous story about the greengrocer who puts the slogan "workers of the world unite" into his shop window, along with the fruits and vegetables, he is highlighting this very fact. Ideology dominated social existence from the slogans repeated daily in the mass media, to the language that had to be used to get on with all sorts of bureaucratic activities. Previously existing socialism was permeated with scarcities, from housing to schooling, to traveling. Applications for relief required proof of ideological commitment. Wanting a vacation or permission to visit family abroad: ideological soundness was required. Seeking entrance into the university, looking for an apartment, wanting to move into a major city, again: ideological soundness was required. Membership in the Communist Party was a sure way to demonstrate soundness, not being religious, taking part in "voluntary" work for the good of the society, and having the correct social class background, using the official language in public and in applications were among the ways of demonstrating ideological soundness. Crucially, as I have already indicated, belief in the ideology was less important than the appearance of the ideology through its language. This facilitated everyday actions as it legitimated the system.

c. *Grounds for social mobilization:* Arendt notes a different type of power, the power of people acting in concert. This points to the possibilities of resistance, as we will see below, but it also accounts for how ideological power is sustained. Using the ideology not only informed individuals as they interacted with each other, legitimating the terms of their interaction, but also facilitated concerted action, even when the action was directed against the ruling authorities. The regime established all sorts of organizations to realize its mission. Among expert critical observers of Communist systems many of these were called "conveyor belts," in the sense that they brought the party ideology to all sorts of locations throughout the society. Trade unions, student organizations, ancillary political parties, professional associations, community centers, Cultural Houses, among many others, acted as such conveyors. But they were actually more than this. In these locations, the ideology enabled and organized social action. These institutional forms were central to the everyday political culture, a key to the viability of the ideological order, and they were also arenas of vulnerability. Cultural Houses, for example, were to be found throughout the Soviet bloc and in China, in small towns, as well as in city neighborhoods. Reading groups, theater, music and dance productions, movies, poetry readings, along with explicit activities of ideological indoctrination were among the activities in these Cultural Houses. They brought people together who had common interests. They were officially approved public spaces. This was of special significance because a great deal of official policy restricted public gathering, especially in the evenings, that was not officially organized. People met each other in these places, with the official intention of following the official script, the ruling ideology. It was here that they could act together.

The ideology empowered, defining the (regime) truth, as it provided the basis of legitimation and as it organized people's capacity to meet and act together. Marxism lived as truth, as opposed to ideology, wedded with power to form a distinct truth regime. And it lived as an ideology embattled with other ideologies, as it provided legitimation for the Communist-dominated order of things and as it organized and restricted public life. And it is in relation to this three-dimensional account that political culture was reinvented over a long period of time.

The Reinvention of the Truth Regime

1968 was a fateful year for the truth regime of the Soviet bloc.[15] In the famous Prague Spring, the goal was "socialism with a human face." In Poland, students at the University of Warsaw demanded greater academic freedom in the name of realizing socialist ideals, inspired as they were by their Marxist humanist teachers, such as Adam Schaff, Zygmunt Bauman, and Leszek Kołakowski. The way the students in Warsaw and then throughout Poland, criticized the order of things, and the way the Prague Spring developed as an attempt to liberalize socialism were classic. They had many manifestations throughout the Soviet bloc, including the thaw in the Soviet Union following Stalin's death and the post-Stalinist developments throughout the old bloc. Marxist ideology was used as a measure against socialist realities, and alternative ways of doing things were put forward. In such a way, market innovations were proposed as a new form of socialist planning. Nationalism was added to the ideological repertoire, as the *Polish, Romanian,* and *Hungarian* road to socialism. And liberal reforms were included in cultural policies to enhance the glory of socialist culture. Such flexibility was sometimes a result of intentional policy, more often a result of the dynamics of social life.

As official policy, the leaders of Poland developed a Polish road.[16] After 1956, with the ascendance of Władysław Gomułka as the head of the Communist Party, a kind of détente was established between the Catholic Church and the party and with Polish peasants. The party stopped pursuing an aggressive atheistic posture, and it called to a halt the collectivization of the agricultural sector. Cultural policy also was significantly opened. All of this was done in the name of a distinctively national characteristic of socialism.

In Hungary also after 1956, a distinctive approach to socialism was developed, so called *Goulash Communism* or *Kadarism*.[17] After the revolution against the Stalinist regime was brutally repressed, party leader Janos Kadar in the 1960s slowly opened the economy to market innovations, tolerating an expanding private sector, and loosened censorship. Discontent with the regime was placated through a slow improvement in living conditions, especially in comparison to Hungary's socialist neighbors.

In Romania, the audience for reforms was more the international community, less the Romanian people (Tismaneanu, 2003).

As a way of securing party dominance, Nicolae Ceausescu chartered an independent foreign policy. He committed the nation to "independent socialist development," refused Romanian participation in the Warsaw Pact invasion of Czechoslovakia, and maintained diplomatic relations with Israel. Coupled with this foreign policy independent from the Soviet Union and the other socialist nations of the bloc was a harsh Stalinist domestic policy: tight cultural controls, austere economic policies, the destruction of historic Bucharest to make way for monumental socialist building projects, along with the destruction of rural communities to make way for forced urbanization of the countryside.

The policies of the Communist parties of Poland, Hungary, and Romania could not have been more different. However, from our point of view, considering the dynamics of political culture, they shared a common ideological configuration. In each, distinctive policy was presented as being drawn from a commitment to official Marxism. They were manifestations of a party line. The truth of the party forms the policy; the policy confirms the party's truth. When Trotsky was still a loyal Bolshevik, he declared the way this works: "We can only be right with and by the Party, for history has provided no other way of being in the right" (quoted in Arendt, 1968: 307). This is the true meaning of political correctness.

The primary challenge for those who were committed to different policies or judgments about social or cultural affairs, was to justify them with reference to the same ideology, to show that they were "correct." Big and small politics, on center stage and in everyday life, those who after the fact appear to be progressive and regressive, used the official ideology to confirm the correctness of their position. This included many surprises. Among those who played the game of the truth regime were innovative artists, such as Jerzy Grotowski (a Communist Party member) who was one of the great theatrical innovators of the twentieth century, who created a mystical "poor theater" drawing on the metaphysics of classic myths, the Bible, and Dostoievsky (see Kumiega, 1987; Grotowski, 2002; Richards, 1995), and reactionary politicians, such as Bolesław Piasecki, an inter-war fascist, who in the post-war period presented himself as the head of PAX, the progressive

Catholic organization, which in the name of progress pursued his inter-war ultra-nationalist agenda (see Blit, 1965; Kunicki, 2005). And within the party, it included those who challenged those in power both from liberal and nationalist angles, in 1968 in Poland including progressives such as Jacek Kuroń and Karol Modzelewski and reactionary nationalists such as the head of a major veterans' association, General Mieczysław Moczar (Kuroń and Modzelewski, 1968).[18] Each side used official ideology to account for the correctness of its position, and the truth of its positions was confirmed or disconfirmed by the outcome of intra-party struggles.

But this dynamic was not only about dramatic events, as in 1968, and grand projects of the avant garde and the politically exotic. It was also built into normal institutionalized social life, in which those who needed to get on with their professional and personal lives had to utilize the official ideology, the official truth, to do so. Artists and scientists, students and professors, lawyers and workers would try to define their projects as inspired by the official ideology in order to get on with these projects in their own way. The theater world I observed in the early seventies was built upon this strategy, as was a broad range of independent cultural expression throughout the Soviet bloc.

In the case of the theater, the use of ideology was knitted into the organizational support of the theaters, it was incorporated into their theater performances, and was an ongoing aspect of the negotiations between the makers of the theater and the political authorities.

The Polish Socialist Student Association supported the theaters. Its mission was to support Polish students in socialist society. It supported a broad range of social and cultural activities, all of which were supposed to support students and contribute to the making of socialism in Poland. The association was originally founded in the post-war period as the Polish Student Organization. It was only after 1968, in the early seventies, that it took on the new name and a more explicit ideological function. Nonetheless, it was exactly at this time, when the authorities had escalated the ideological demands on the association, that it came to support theater that was to an unprecedented degree both aesthetically innovative and politically challenging (Goldfarb, 1980). The work was very far from the kind of ideological art and propaganda that Lenin's notion of party-supported culture envisaged or that was common fare during Stalinist times in the Soviet Union and Soviet bloc. Significantly, though, it was justified as being informed by Marxism and the making of a socialist society, and to some extent, this may even have been the case.

The organization demanded politically correct cultural work, and the theater groups explained their work in these terms. They presented work that was radically different from that which officialdom would want, but they did so using the language of officialdom. This was the art of socialist youth, "engaged theater." Far from being anti-socialist, the theaters presented themselves as pro-socialist. Many in the movement used this language to get on with their critical innovative art, not really believing the official rhetoric that allowed for their work, but others sincerely believed the rhetoric. So when I was asked whether this theater was pro or anti regime, socialist or anti-socialist, when I returned from my research, I had a hard time answering this question. The theaters were committed to independent cultural and political positions, but they accounted for themselves using the language of the official truth.

At the same time that this was happening, something quite distinct was developing among more forceful political critics of the regime. For them, ideology was ending. For such critics, 1968 marked the beginning of the end of ideology around the Soviet bloc. That was the year, particularly in Poland and Czechoslovakia, that Marxism was last used by the radical critics of the previously existing socialist order, using the official ideology to promote fundamental change. Yet, it was not just a matter of turning from one ideology and choosing another. A long cultural march was required to change the political culture. The type of relationship between power and culture was even more significant than the political and cultural commitments of the critics. These commitments were quite similar to the student theaters and other cultural developments that existed on the margins of the officially accepted.

But they started to articulate their commitments without using the official language. They stopped gaming with the censor, started to speak in a clear and non-ideological language. Adam Michnik's notion of acting as if they lived in a free society and Vaclav Havel's notion of living in truth, both already mentioned, summarized the strategy that was being put into practice. Poland was the center of such activity, although similar things were being done in Hungary and Czechoslovakia. In the early seventies, a self-organized opposition was constituted.

A group of intellectuals, and then intellectuals together with industrial workers took steps that did not utilize the ruling ideology as an explanation and justification of their actions. In 1974 and 1975, there was a protest in Poland against changes in the constitution that formally recognized the party's hegemonic role and the Soviet Party's leadership position in the building of socialism. People actually organized among themselves against the party's vanguard status, a key Leninist position, and they did so without reference to official ideology. This detachment from the ideology anticipated major changes in the political culture.

In 1976, there was a nationwide strike protesting food price increases. The party headquarters in the city of Radom was attacked and burnt down. Workers in Ursus, just outside of Warsaw, tore up the railroad tracks, which connected the corridor between the Soviet Union and Germany. Many of the workers involved were fired and imprisoned. This type of large-scale revolt occurred previously in Poland, in 1956 in Poznań and in 1970 in Gdańsk. It also is the kind of revolt that occurred occasionally throughout the Soviet bloc. But then something quite unusual happened. A group of intellectuals formed the Committee to Defend Workers (KOR). They arranged for legal defense for those charged with crimes. They established a kind of welfare system, collecting funds to support the workers' families. They publicized their own activities in a *Bulletin of Information* (using the title of an underground publication from the times of the Polish partition), and then went on to publish a broad range of political and literary texts, bulletins, magazines, and books (Lipski, Moore, and Amsterdamska, 1985).

Crucially, all of this activity was done in the open. It was public. The names, addresses, and telephone numbers of those involved were published. All the publications were illegal, but just about all the leaders in this movement acted openly, they were not dissidents. Their work was not in a strict sense "underground." Both the form and the content of their actions actively separated truth and power, actively challenged the truth regime.

Workers started organizing themselves, culminating in the creation of *Solidarność* – Solidarity – a broad nationwide movement that presented itself as a simple trade union, throughout its history both above and below ground. The union addressed the concerns of workers and a broad segment of the population in concrete terms. Its great significance was that it was completely independent of the ruling party and did not use its ideology in pursuing its goal. It filled a vacuum and became the movement representing such independence not only for workers, but also for society as a whole. It was not against the ruling order, but apart from it. This principle of action built on social networks and cultural activities that emerged from the KOR group, and then, when Solidarity was illegal, after the declaration of martial law, the Solidarity underground systematically supported those same networks and activities in a greatly expanded way.

Solidarity, both above and below ground, stood in contrast to the party's operation as a truth regime, as it turned away from engaging in ideological battle. Its actions were neither Marxist nor anti-Marxist. The character of the movement is best revealed in the Gdansk Agreement's provisions which resulted from a nationwide strike in August 1980 that led to the formation of Solidarity.

The Twenty-One Demands of the workers agreed to by the Communist officials were:

1. Free trades unions independent from the party and employers are accepted as provided by Convention 87 of the International Labour Organisation on free trades unions ratified by the Polish People's Republic.
2. The right to strike as well as safety of those on strike and their supporters is guaranteed.

3. Freedom of speech and freedom to print and publish are guaranteed as provided by the Constitution of the Polish People's Republic; that independent publishing houses are not persecuted; and that mass media are made available to the representatives of all denominations.

4. a) The workers sacked after the strikes of 1970 and 1976 are allowed to return to work; students expelled from universities for their convictions are allowed to return to schools.
   b) All political prisoners are released (including Edmund Zadrożyński, Jan Kozłowski, and Marek Kozłowski).
   c) Persecution for convictions is abolished.

5. Information about the creation of MKS (the strike committee) is made public in the media together with the demands.

6. Activities are undertaken to lead the country out of the crisis through:
   a) Informing the general public about the real political and economic situation in the country.
   b) Allowing all social groups and strata to take part in a discussion about the program of reforms.

7. All workers taking part in the strike are paid remuneration from the budget of CRZZ (the Central Council of Trades Unions) for the period on strike as if they were on leave.

8. All workers receive a pay rise of 2,000 zlotys per month as compensation for price rises.

9. Wages are increased automatically with any price rises or zloty devaluation.

10. The internal market is fully supplied with food and that only surplus food is exported.

11. The commercial prices and foreign currency trade in the so-called internal export are abolished.

12. Managers are selected according to their skills and not party membership and that special privileges for police, secret service personnel, and party members are abolished through:
    – The introduction of equal family benefits;
    – The abolition of privileged purchasing etc.

13. Food coupons for meat and processed food are introduced (until the situation on the food market has become stable).

14. Retirement age is lowered for women to 50 years of age and for men to 55 years or alternatively retirement after having worked in the Polish People's Republic for 30 years for women and 35 years for men regardless of age.
15. Old age and disability pensions, which are calculated according to the old rules, are made equal with those paid at present.
16. Working conditions of health-care workers are improved which will result in full medical care for those who work.
17. That working mothers are provided with enough places in nurseries and kindergartens.
18. A three-year paid maternity leave is introduced for bringing up children.
19. Waiting time for apartments is shortened.
20. Travel allowances are increased from 40 zlotys to 100 zlotys and that a separation benefit is introduced.
21. All Saturdays are free. Employees working in the four-shift system will be compensated with longer leaves or other free days for which they will be paid. (Polish State Archives, 1980)

There is much that is noteworthy about this list of demands. That it was accepted by a ruling Communist Party in retrospect points to the great transformations of 1989.

The form rather than the substance of the demands was most revolutionary. It marked the end of the Marxist-Leninist truth regime. There was no attempt to justify the positions with reference to official ideology. Simple straightforward issues were involved. The right of workers to organize and strike was demanded, not as part of an official teleology, not about building socialism with a human face, using a humanistic Marxism, but as right of self-defense, a right of association, a fundamental human right (items 1 and 2). Also as a human right, freedom of speech was demanded, and those who had suffered for their pursuit of free speech and freedom of assembly were defended (items 3 and 4). There was a concern for open public life, starting with publicity of the strike itself (items 5 and 6). And then there was a list of concrete demands concerning working conditions, pay, and social welfare issues (items 7–21). All these were important for the workers and expressed a very critical attitude toward the organization of political and industrial life in the Polish People's Republic. But the workers and the strike leadership never presented a systemic critique. Indeed throughout its legal period, Lech Wałęsa, the leader of the union, always insisted that Solidarity was not political, but a simple trade union. This famous assertion by Wałęsa was much more complicated than it appears to have been. It seemed to be a strategic conceit, meant to deny the obvious for pragmatic purpose. But more was involved.

In an important way, Wałęsa's claim was true. Solidarity did not want to compete with the Communist Party. It did not cast itself against official ideology. Its leadership and members simply wanted to have some control over their immediate circumstances and have some fundamental rights, which at least formally were granted by the Polish Constitution and by international agreements the Polish party-state had signed (specifically the Helsinki Agreements). This did present a fundamental challenge to the viability of the truth regime, but to understand how this happened requires a closer examination of the politics of legitimation in the long struggle seeking change in the post-war situation.

The Reinvention of Legitimation

With the end of World War II, the political order was more a matter of geo politics than national politics. Given the agreements between the allied powers at the close of war (specifically those reached in Yalta), Poland and the other countries of Eastern Europe were destined to be dominated by the Soviet Union. A few years passed before the Stalinist system was firmly in place. From 1945 until 1948, there was an anti-Communist opposition, but after this period, the only game in town, the only way to effect change was through the Soviet-imposed system using official ideology.

From 1948 until 1956, or so, Stalinism prevailed. Ideology as it legitimated the system of domination, as it established a distinct form of authority in the Weberian sense, worked in the classical totalitarian fashion. It was coupled with terror and explained the party-state-enforced true connection between the past, the present, and the future. Politics was about the party line, in most countries a struggle between Communists who found themselves in the underground during the Nazi occupations, and those who were in exile in Moscow, with the latter dominating. All other political activity was silenced, and even the nationally based Communists were systematically terrorized.

In the mid 1950s, after Stalin's death and after Khrushchev's famous secret speech (Khrushchev, 1956), with the waning of terror, cultural dynamics within the official ideology opened new possibilities in the political culture. People began to creatively explore the possibilities of the given, changing the relationship between power and culture as it fostered new sorts of legitimation. I have already pointed to how this worked in intra-party struggles, the Polish, Hungarian, and Romanian roads to socialism. Even more significant in the long run was how this worked among artists and intellectuals, working beyond party politics.

The most famous case of this is the work of Alexander Solzhenitsyn. For a brief time, he was officially supported and celebrated for his *One Day in the Life of Ivan Denisovich*. He was in a real sense a Soviet author. His work built upon the cultural resources made available through official Soviet cultural policy. He just worked upon the available in creative ways, not anticipated by the Soviet authorities. He drew upon the great novels of the nineteenth century. Tolstoy's novels, for example, were widely distributed by the cultural commissars, even during Stalin's times. As nationalism was incorporated into official cultural policy, these novels were presented as the great works of the national tradition, a critical realism that anticipated the socialist realism of the Soviet twentieth century.[19] But in Solzhenitsyn's imagination, the tradition of the Russian novel provided a means to scathingly reveal the Soviet horrors in the prison camps and beyond. A cultural tradition developed and transformed the relationship between power and culture. While the authorities would use nationalism to empower the state, specifically drawn upon during World War II, the national literary tradition was creatively utilized to attack this legitimacy. An enemy of state was born using the cultural resources made available by the socialist state.

More straightforwardly, the claims of socialist accomplishments were contrasted with socialist realities. At the first production of Polish youth theater I observed, the production which introduced me to the movement and suggested to me the focus of my original research in Eastern Europe, in *Retrospekywa*, a banquet was depicted. The audience entered the student club on 77 Piotrkowska Street. As we found places to sit down on the periphery of a very large room, members of the audience started talking to us. They complained about the problems of everyday life, food prices and shortages, finding an apartment, getting their child into a pre-school, or a proper doctor for an ill relative. In the meanwhile in the center of the room, speeches were given, calling for the solidarity of workers, drawing fine distinctions between the evils of cosmopolitanism and the great promise of internationalism. Theater 77 was presenting one of the classic forms of critical work common throughout the old Soviet bloc.

Such work included the sophomoric and the very limited, as well as great art. Sometimes it seemed to function as a kind of socialist repressive tolerance, at other times it went far beyond ideological games. When the work had enduring value, it pointed beyond narrow ideological politics. But even when it was not profound, it presented alternatives. The great Russian theater of the early twentieth century, the theater of Meyerhold and Stanislavsky, was all but killed during the Stalinist era. The challenging theater that remained did not go much beyond challenging the censor within a very narrow range.[20] But even in this case, some challenges were forthcoming and people could meet in theaters to confirm their commitment to the challenge, making society different from one where such challenges do not exist, e.g., Stalin's Soviet Union.

Such difference was much greater when the cultural works reached beyond the local ideological struggles and spoke to broader concerns. This changed the nature of the political culture. The example I studied closely was Polish theater, but such was the case in the rich artistic world of "the other Europe" during the Communist period. In the films of Andrzej Wajda, Krzysztof

Kieślowski, Miloš Forman, Ján Kadár and Elmar Klos and Miklós Jancsó, and the novels of George Konrad, Milan Kundera, Bohumil Hrabal, Danilo Kiš, Tadeusz Konwicki, Jerzy Andrzejewski, and Tadeusz Borowski, the problems of the modern human condition are depicted and reflected upon, despite censorship and official prescriptions about what proper socialist art should be.[21] Film, theater, novels, and poetry of great quality became available, some quite excellent and often superior to contemporary work on the other side of the *Iron Curtain*. That these refined works existed alongside the world as understood by the official ideology enriched the cultural life of previously existing socialism, challenging the political order, changing the political culture. When they passed censorship and reached a broad audience, the political order changed. On the one hand, the authorities gained legitimacy because they presided over a cultural world that included such works. The authorities could use their tolerance for aesthetic independence to show their advanced nature and the maturity of the socialist order. On the other hand, these works stood in contrast with the limitations of the world according to officialdom, according to the official ideology – just as the conversations the actors of Theater 77 had with audience members stood in contrast to the hackneyed official speeches given at the banquet.

The politics of legitimation, then, with the end of terror occurred within the party and beyond. Within the party it was a manifestation of intra-party conflicts. In society at large, there were struggles to extend the range of cultural works and social activities officially permitted. The consequence of the former suggested how liberal and how nationalist the party-state would be. The consequence of the latter extended the intra-party consequences, but also had a capacity to go beyond them, taking many different paths, following the light of creativity of cultural expression and social action. Because the legitimation politics was not only about intra-party struggles and their consequences, there was the possibility of vibrancy and openness in the political culture of previously existing socialist states. The appearance of independent work supported by the official order was the source of legitimacy of the regimes, thus the liberal legitimacy of Czechoslovakia before the Soviet invasion in 1968, and the liberal legitimacy of the Polish and Hungarian parties through the seventies. On the other hand, the openness could lend legitimacy to critics of the official line of the moment, leading to calls for greater liberalism or greater nationalism on the part of party factions and significant segments of the population. This notably occurred in Czechoslovakia and Poland in 1968.

Yet, despite the openness and uncertainty, despite the alternative histories evident around the bloc, all of this happened within the existing order, not against it, pointing beyond it culturally in creative works, but not politically in action. This would require a completely different political game, the move that the Polish opposition and Solidarity made, secession from the official order. This, in fact, is what lies behind Wałęsa's simple assertion that Solidarity is not a political organization, that it is just trade union. He was maintaining the union's secession from the politics of legitimation of the official order. He was reinventing the political culture. The most radical political challenge was to be anti-political. This move had its basis in the everyday life of just about everyone in the socialist order.

Reinventing Social Mobilization: "The Politics of Small Things"

The performance *Retrospekywa* realistically depicted the sociology of language in the everyday life of previously existing socialism. In the center of the room, the actors gave official speeches. On the sidelines, other actors used ordinary language, privately in hushed tones, to complain about their circumstances and problems. Such a distinction between formal public discourse and informal private talk is common. But it played a special role in previously existing socialism. Particularly significant was how people used private meetings and informal language to respond to the demands of the official public order. There was an irony. People were able to freely meet each other, tell stories, sometimes of an everyday sort, but also about history as it was personally experienced, only in private places. In such places, people together reflected upon the meaning of current events and discussed how they should act. Only in these private places, were they able to form free publics. It was around the kitchen table where people were able to freely talk about their public concerns (see Goldfarb, 2006). There was a material base for the reinvention of political culture. The fundamental breakthroughs involved the detachment of truth from the party-state and the broadening of the terms of legitimation, as we have just observed. But these required a social basis for political mobilization, independent of the regime. This had to do with everyday struggles.

During Stalinist times, people met and spoke in public in highly restricted ways. Even in Poland with its very strong Catholic Church, religious institutions were under attack. Various social groups were either supported by the party-state on its terms, or closed down. Political parties, a prime example, were re-formed, co-opted as ancillary Communist parties, incorporated into the ruling party, or repressed. Neighborhood associations, women's groups, scouting, labor unions, etc. were affiliated and controlled by the powers, or shut down. This was an extension of Lenin's notion of ideological struggle. Collectivization of private property, from farms to major corporations led to almost complete party-state control over economic life. This had striking economic consequences, improving working conditions for many, undermining economic circumstances for others. But beyond the political, cultural, and economic consequences of all these changes, they most fundamentally changed the way people could associate with each other. Broadly speaking, public association existed through the party-state apparatus, or not at all. Thus the great significance of the informal interactions of friends and family around the kitchen table and other private places where people who trusted each other could speak without the official scripts, about anything and everything. There were instances of party attempts to control the kitchen table, getting children to inform on their parents, but these were relatively rare and ineffective. The confinement of free informal interaction fundamentally defined the political culture. Its expansion meant fundamental change, the reinvention of political culture.

I write about the kitchen table as a real social phenomenon, but also as a metaphor that points beyond the specific location. In the privacy of the home, with the most trusted family and friends, people living in totalitarian circumstances dared to say what was on their minds. They told forbidden truths about personal experiences that belied official accounts of public events, e.g., about the family inheritance lost, the imprisonment or exile suffered, the premature death in the family. And they tried to make sense of current policies. What did it mean that a party leader retired because of "sickness of the eyes" after riots followed his failed attempt to increase food prices?[22] What did it say about party policy that an extremely candid portrayal of life in the Gulag passed censorship and was published (Solzhenitsyn, 1963)? What is the significance of the demotion of a local party official and the promotion of another? Such decisions were accounted for using official ideology in the official press, but their significance for ordinary people was far from clear from the official account. People had to discuss with each other the meaning of the official account in order to get on with their lives, in fact, even in order to fulfill their official responsibilities. This happened around the kitchen table, but, as well, in all sorts of informal discussions in which people discussed among themselves how to adapt to the circumstances. Some of these discussions would happen among true believers, people committed to the order of things, as well as among people disdainful of the order. Both sorts of people needed to take part in such discussions.

If someone did not get a promotion in a factory and was told by a supervisor that this was because he needed to reveal more civic engagement, friends and colleagues would discuss among themselves the cause of the predicament. Even someone in authority might use an informal situation to explain. Was it because the person was not a party member, or did not attend the May Day celebration or was too openly active in Church or the like? People had to figure out with each other what was permitted and what was not; which sort of discouraged activities would be consequential and which would not be; why a particularly challenging essay would pass censorship, and why another one would not; what kind of research was permitted, what kind was encouraged, and what kind was beyond the bounds. Such discussions helped people get on with their lives, and they also were necessary for official institutions to function. Only if people understood the situation with some clarity among themselves could they enact the party line and exercise their official responsibilities. Ultimately, in order for the leaders to rule, the party leaders in the center of the performance of *Retrospekywa* needed to make some sense to the people off the center stage who speak to each other in hushed tones. The kitchen table, metaphorically speaking, was a functional structure of the prevailing political order. Its culture was a necessary aspect of the ruling order, although an aspect that did not only yield supportive results.

The kitchen table was the social setting where transformation was always a possibility, and it was the expansion of free and open discussion that was typical of informal gatherings to less informal ones, ones less dependent upon bonds of intimacy, that marked fundamental change. The party-state controlled public life, but free publics could be formed in the ubiquitous settings of informal interaction. This became the basis of a social mobilization outside the networks of the party-state. This was the social material of the reinvention of political culture.

When the truth regime of the party-state prevailed, when legitimation of ideology was operative, the development of autonomous public action was circumscribed. People would use the capacity to independently speak and act within the prevailing order. The simple existence of such action changed the nature of the system, but the system prevailed. The real change occurred when such action no longer was so circumscribed, when Havel's greengrocers of the world united and together omitted to put up the sign "workers of the world unite" in their shop windows along with the fruits and vegetables.

As I attempted to explain to my professor, Morris Janowitz, the simple existence of alternative theater changed the nature of the Communist system in Poland. Through these theaters, theatrical experimentation became a part of the normal life of a fundamentally repressive society. In these theaters, among the performers and the audience, alternative sensibilities and accounts of experience could be shared. Embedded in the formal institutions was an alternative though delimited public space. But this type of social action was hardly confined to these theaters. In the arts and sciences generally, in the university and the various academies, people interacted with each other in informal publics to support activities that had political independence and professional authority that was apart from that of the party-state. They worked against censorship and political interference, doing so in organized ways.

In my discipline of sociology, for example, scholars worked on a distinctive Polish sociological tradition independent from official Marxism.[23] The starting point of this tradition was the work of Florian Znaniecki, followed by the heroic efforts of Stanisław Ossowski and Maria Ossowska, and the solid sociology of such leading figures as Jan Szczepański, Jerzy Szacki, Stefan Nowak, Jerzy Wiatr, Włodzimierz Wesołowski, Jan Strzelecki, and Zygmunt Bauman. These were independent thinkers and researchers, some active political actors in the party-state, others quite critical of it. But they shared a commitment to the integrity of sociology as an independent discipline. In their daily interactions, they affirmed this independence. The Ossowskis actually held a regular meeting in their private apartment which kept sociology alive when it was disbanded at the height of Stalinism (from 1951 to 1956). The others were instrumental in working in the Polish Sociological Association, using it to maintain the discipline's independence and the vitality of various currents of sociological theory and research. The association was originally founded in 1931, one of the first associations in Europe. After the war and Stalinism, it was re-founded in 1957, one of the signs of the end of Stalinism. Poorly funded, subject to indirect control, it nonetheless managed to be a center of independent research, political discussion, and scholarly exchange. In this association, members of the Academy of Sciences and the universities had another venue to meet and discuss their work, one that allowed less constrained interaction, with clearer focus on scientific autonomy. And the interaction in the association affected what happened at the university and the academy. The work done in the association did not have direct political effect. On the other hand, its work did sustain a significant intellectual tradition, which flourished after the changes of 1989. The nature of social science research and teaching at the time of the changes and since has been different in Poland than in many other countries in the post-Communist situation. This is largely due to the interactions among the members of the Polish Sociological Association.

The radical transformation of the political culture occurred when such interactions completely severed their ties with the ideological order. Solidarity as just a trade union was the great case in point. But there were many smaller ones. One of the major opposition activities of the seventies was "The Flying University." In it, social science and history of the recent past were taught in private apartments at scheduled times, free from the constraints of censorship and party-state surveillance. Key controversial topics such as the Katyń massacre, the history of the Home Army (the non-Communist resistance), key critical events in recent Polish history, 1956, 1968, 1970, 1976, when popular resistance emerged and was repressed, were examined. This "Society of Scientific Courses," as it was alternatively called, essentially formally taught what previously was only passed on around the kitchen table, including the tables where members of the Polish Sociological Association met. The "Society of Scientific Courses" had a publicized schedule, with known lecturers and confirmed "classrooms." The public life that was hidden came out in the open.

Even more impressive was the development of an independent publishing system. It started with the publication of *The Bulletin of Information*, a newsletter that reported on the work of the Committee to Defend Workers, (KOR). The committee used *The Bulletin* to publicize the situation of workers arrested in the aftermath of the workers' revolt in 1976. They reported on their legal cases, attempted to raise funds for their defense and for the support of their families. It reported on the twists and turns of official policies and the opposition's response. In brief, *The Bulletin* reported on the information that previously was only reported and discussed around the kitchen table. But crucially, they addressed themselves to a broad anonymous audience, and they did so publishing the names, addresses, and telephone numbers of those involved in the oppositional activity. From this humble beginning, people of like minds and common concerns started to publish and distribute a broad range of periodicals of various sorts and eventually books. An entire underground cultural system developed, including journals of arts and letters: *Zapis* (the first such publication), *Spotkania*, and *Puls*; political journals from the left, *Krytyk*; and the right, *Res Publica,* and independent publishing houses such as NOW-a, the first and most prominent of many. In the 1980s, after the declaration of martial law, sustaining this alternative system became a major activity of the Solidarity underground. This activity is a perfect example of the notion of political power as developed by Arendt. People met each other, spoke in each others' presence, and acted in concert, transforming Polish society and culture. The publication reach of the independent cultural system rivaled the official system. There was an elaborate system of production, distribution, and sales. Authors, publishers, printers, and booksellers actually earned income, for some a living wage. And the published work was not legitimated using the official ideology, and it explicitly offered works that were distinct from the official truth. The system was not set against the party-state apparatus, but independent from it. They brought, as Arendt would describe it, "something new into the world."

I saw this first hand. In 1985, I co-founded with Adam Michnik an international seminar investigating the political and culture. In some ways, this book is a continuation of the discussions we had back then. This was a minor initiative, but it did provide a bird's-eye view, which can be applied to understanding the interactive basis of the alternative cultural world. The seminar was a typical opposition activity, actually quite modest in design and immediately successful because the means of the seminar was its goal. That the seminar participants managed to interact with each other at all was its great success. The plan was to establish an international conversation about democratic theory and practice. The starting point of the conversation would be one that Michnik and I began when we first got to know each other.

I was in Warsaw in December 1984 to take part in an unofficial ceremony granting him an honorary degree from my university, the New School for Social Research. I met him the day before the event, which took place in a private apartment with a broad collection of opposition figures and Jonathan Fanton, the President of the New School and Adrian Dewind, a member of our Board of Trustees and his wife. I stayed a week after the ceremony, talking to Michnik, meeting his friends and colleagues, being introduced to the opposition scene. Adam and I spoke around his living room table and the kitchen tables of scholars, intellectuals, and artists of Warsaw, and also in the hospital of Jan Józef Lipski, then a patient at the cardiac hospital on the outskirts of the city.

We went to the hospital the day after the ceremony. Michnik wanted to share with the respected opposition historian his excitement over the honorary degree (an excitement that really surprised me). They spoke about Lipski's recent research on inter-war fascism in Poland. We spoke about the significance of the Pope for independent-minded Poles, both workers and intellectuals. This was one of the many conversations Michnik and I had about contemporary history, politics, and political theory. One fascination we shared was in the philosophy and political theory of Hannah Arendt. We also spoke about common friends in Hungary and Czechoslovakia. Upon leaving the hospital, Michnik turned to me and proposed, the seminar idea, "now that we are New School colleagues." Vaclav Havel in Prague, György Bence in Budapest, he in Warsaw, and I in New York would organize parallel seminars on the topics we had been discussing during my visit. The starting point of the discussions would be Hannah Arendt's *The Origins of Totalitarianism*. Each group would read a common assignment, exchange summaries of the proceedings and propose further study. From 1985 through 1989, the seminar functioned in Budapest, New York, and Warsaw. Political conditions made the seminar impossible in Prague. The Polish sociologist Jerzy Szacki chaired the Warsaw seminar because three months after our agreement Michnik was again imprisoned, charged with treason. There were many twists and turns in the seminar, many interesting discussions, and some significant exchanges. It continued to function into the 1990s across the former Soviet bloc (Matynia, 1996). Noteworthy from our point of view is that it was a setting for the reinvention of political culture, indeed it was a material manifestation of the reinvention. It mobilized interaction in a different way. It was a center for the critical but dispassionate examination of the official truth, and it was clearly set apart from official ideology.

Conclusions

Official Marxism ordered previously socialist societies. The official ideology was knitted into all aspects of society. There was an official truth and it was applied across the board. Authority was legitimated, albeit sometimes in very odd ways, using Marxism. And the structure of social interaction was formed by institutional arrangements informed by the official ideology. With the collapse of the Berlin Wall and the events surrounding the collapse, this all ended. But change was not as sudden and miraculous as has often been imagined. As we have examined in this chapter, there was a long, complex cultural march that supported the "sudden" transformation. Political culture was reinvented in ways that had lasting results for those immediately involved in the former Soviet bloc, but also beyond these and those times. Deliberately over a long period of time, the truth regime was dismantled, the ideology was turned against itself, and then discarded, and the means for collectively acting beyond the truth regime and the ideology were established. In the end, a very different political culture emerged, one that has proven to be supportive of democracy in the post-Communist situation.

The fundamental insight of the transformative political culture was the need, as a matter of principle, to detach truth from power, to secede from the ideological order, as a truth regime, a form of legitimation, and as a structure of everyday practice. This insight stands in clear opposition to Foucault's understanding of the nature of the relationship between truth and power, the notion that they are intimately connected in one truth regime or another. The political cultural practice in opposition to the

Marxist-Leninist state was dedicated to refuting this very notion. The position of the post-Communist political culture stood with Marx in opposition to the Leninist notion of ideology, that ideas are weapons wielded by one group against another, serving class interests. But against Marx, long experience with the philosophy of the working class, which official Marxism claimed to have, told oppositionists that such a class affiliation was far from a basis of truth. Rather, the official truth, in the eyes of the leading intellectuals and political activists of the former Soviet bloc, such as those who took part in our Democracy Seminar, was revealed to be the big lie. The philosophical task, then, but also the practical one, was to detach truth and various sorts of social commitments from the powers. Practically that meant being engaged in independent social activities such as the Democracy Seminar, alternative publishing, and the Flying University. Solidarity was the culmination of such practical action. The practical project of these social activities was to act independently and openly in ways that were not connected to the regime. The project for theorists was to spell this out conceptually, beautifully accomplished in the writings of Adam Michnik and Vaclav Havel, among many others (see especially Michnik, 1987, and Havel, 1985). The project was to end ideology, a major transformation in the political culture.

There is much that is noteworthy and that is lasting in the transformation, but also much that has proven to be disappointing. Euphoria followed the fall of the Berlin Wall, when observers and participants alike had very high expectations about the transition to democracy. There were those who thought that with the changes a Western-style democracy, with Western prosperity, was just around the corner. Events transpired to indicate how difficult such a change would be. Others thought that the victory of Solidarity and the wonders of the Velvet Revolutions would lead finally to a third way between capitalism and socialism, with "real democracy." I had my doubts (Goldfarb, 1992). I knew that an established liberal democracy would not emerge as an end to history, nor would there be a democratic alternative to capitalism, and a non-bureaucratic alternative to socialism was also not on the near horizon, to say the least. But I have to admit I also had my false hopes. I thought that the political culture described in this chapter would yield more immediate and lasting results than has proven to be the case. There was a remarkable reinvention of political culture, but its impact was uneven and sometimes quite shallow.

I thought that the era of magical modern politics, the ideological era, was becoming a thing of the past. I thought that a kind of global collective learning had occurred in the aftermath of the horrors of the twentieth century. I thought that the great failures of the totalitarian left and right would extinguish totalitarian temptations. I did not anticipate the degree to which various forms of nationalism and xenophobia in previously existing socialist societies would be used to address the difficult problems that the people of the former Soviet bloc would have to address. I did not then understand the meaning of Islamist politics and its terrorism, nor the appeal of radical Islamophobia and global anti-terrorism. Instead of the scientism of twentieth-century tyranny, now there is the distortion of religion, (religionism?), which I did not anticipate.[24] I did not imagine the lasting appeal that populism, anti-Americanism, and now a vague socialism would have in Latin America and in other parts of the world.

Yet, even if the collective learning was not as thorough as I had imagined, both in the former Soviet bloc and beyond, the fact remains that there was a new development in political culture. The politics of the opposition to Communism did bring new things into the world. By detaching culture from the powers as a matter of principle, they were able to create two major innovations in our political world (probably among other less major ones), important for them, but also important for those beyond the region. They also centrally highlighted a new anti-ideological sensibility, even if it did not usher in an end of ideology once and for all.

One major innovation was "the round tables" which developed as a means to facilitate the non-violent end to authoritarian and totalitarian regimes around the world to political orders that aspired to be democratic. Originally created in Spain, they played a key role in the post-Soviet world (Matynia, 2001; Peeva, 2000).

A new institutional form has developed that has been applied in a wide variety of different places.

Beyond such organizational specifics, the opposition to previously existing socialism highlighted the significance of a special form of political power: what I have called *the politics of small things*, which has been identified internationally with the colored revolutions. There was a reinvention of political culture as an alternative to prevailing magical ideologies. Each of those revolutions started with political action that detached commitment and judgment from the existing regime, and based political culture on the power of concerted action. While the result is not assured victory, and while the victories achieved were not completely decisive, new political forces have come into being that change the political environment, as Solidarity did in Poland in the 1980s, from Lebanon to Georgia and Ukraine, and, as the authorities deeply fear, on to Iran and the Arab Spring.[25] This sort of power and its culture has even, spectacularly, played a significant role in the transformation of the American scene, as we will observe in the next chapter.

As we proceed below, we will consider the promise of this reinvented political culture as it has developed in our world. We will examine a victory, in the presidential campaign of Barack Obama, and the reaction to that victory that shows its limits, and weigh the prospects in a central deadlocked conflict, between Israel and Palestine. We will examine how a reinvented political culture is challenging prevailing and emerging ideologies, how the power of culture confronts the culture of power, even if the culture does not and cannot vanquish the power.

3

Reinventing American Political Culture: Obama v. Palin

The relationship between power and culture in the United States is strikingly different from the relationship in the former Soviet bloc. Power and culture are not as intimately connected, and as a consequence, the project of de-coupling them at the summit and in the fabric of society is not as compelling. In the former Soviet bloc, there was in fact a truth regime, a regime that enforced an official truth. This concentrated the minds of the entire population. Those who sought change first had to address this fundamental situation. In the worst of times, denying the official truth could lead to imprisonment, or even death. In the best of times, the language of the official truth was required in order to get on with daily life. At all times, the separation of official power and culture was a fundamental critical act. The political culture was constituted between the operation of the truth regime and its critique in its different varieties, as we have seen.

In the United States, and in liberal regimes generally, this is not the case. Things are more complicated. There is not a truth regime in the same sense as that which operated in the former Soviet bloc. Truth and power are not conflated, although they are related. Common sense is the issue, not a truth regime.[26] This is an important distinction to keep in mind as we turn to American political culture and its reinvention. Foucault asserts: "Each society has its regime of truth, its 'general politics' of truth: that is, the types of discourse which it accepts and makes function as true; the mechanisms and instances which enable one to distinguish true and false

71

statements, the means by which each is sanctioned; the techniques and procedures accorded value in the acquisition of truth; the status of those who are charged with saying what counts as true" (Rabinow, 1984: 73).[27] While he is observing that each society has a truth regime, he does not distinguish between truth regimes and other political cultural arrangements linking culture with power. I think that that distinction is crucial.

In the US, common sense is a powerful force (Geertz, 1983). This Tocqueville observed in *Democracy in America*. As we noted in the opening of our inquiry, he illuminated how Americans have a distinctive "philosophic approach." He was not observing an enforced truth, but a prevailing common sense, which he saw as being a consequence of democracy itself. A democratic form of governance is intimately connected to egalitarian social attitudes and relations. Indeed, these attitudes and this form of governance are mutually related and constituting. The attitudes and form of governance support and are supported by individualism, which yields a skeptical, anti-authoritarian philosophy, a modern Cartesian philosophy, even though Americans, as Tocqueville ironically observed, do not read Descartes. This has consequences. They develop not as inevitable process, but as the result of interaction. A field of democratic culture is opened, with many contradictions, possibilities, and dangers.

American political culture, American power and culture related, has great promise and presents great perils, as the dramatic twists and turns in our history reveal, and as Tocqueville himself discovered at the beginning of the nineteenth century. There are the general problems, such as the relationship between individual interests and calculation, and the common good (in contemporary discussions liberalism versus communitarianism) (Tocqueville, 2000: 479–521), and the nature of political participation (180–6). And there are specific political cultural challenges: the problems of race (302–98), and the relationships between capitalism and democracy (530–4), church and state (417–25), and between judgments of quality and egalitarianism (428–78). These are ongoing challenges that Tocqueville recognized as emerging from democratic society and its culture, and that have defined American political culture for centuries. But these challenges have been addressed and transformed. They do not simply persist. They are interactively constituted and reconstituted (Eliasoph, 1998). In interaction, the culture and politics are related, and reinvention of political culture becomes possible.

Such possibility has been striking in recent years. The major narratives about national and political identity have been developed in innovative ways both by political leaders and ordinary people in everyday practices. Both the change and resistance to the change over common sense and the means of politically enacting the changes and their resistance have been worked on. In this chapter, we examine this by considering how Barack Obama told a different version of the American story and how there has been a concerted rejection of this retelling. We will then analyze the ways the retold story and the rejection have been enacted in social interaction, first how each side has innovatively utilized a new form of the politics of small things, and then how each side has developed new ways of persuasion in the media environment including the internet, talk radio, and cable TV news. Both through the media and through everyday interactions, power has been culturally constituted and culture has been empowered.

Changing Common Sense

During the campaign for the Democratic Party's nomination for President of the United States in 2008, Obama expressed, in an interview with the editorial board of a Nevada newspaper, his admiration for Ronald Reagan:

> I think Ronald Reagan changed the trajectory of America in a way that Richard Nixon did not and in a way that Bill Clinton did not. He put us on a fundamentally different path because the country was ready for it. I think they [the American public] felt like with all the excesses of the 1960s and 1970s and government had grown and grown but there wasn't much sense of accountability in terms of how it was operating. I think people, he just tapped into what people were

already feeling, which was we want clarity, we want optimism, we want a return to that sense of dynamism and entrepreneurship that had been missing.[28]

Although this admiration was very controversial during the campaign, it clearly reveals his political grounding. Not a rightist, not a leftist, he is an imaginative centrist. He is not committed to a strong partisan stance. He wants open public debate among people with different positions, but he wants to turn the terms of the debate. He seeks to reinvent the political center, as Reagan did, and as Roosevelt did before him, as Bill Clinton and Richard Nixon did not.

Roosevelt convinced Americans by his rhetoric and policies that public resources should be used to address problems of the "private" economy – this, significantly, in the middle of the Great Depression when people knew that there was something fundamentally wrong with the existing state of affairs. He introduced a basic social safety net into American life, from unemployment insurance to social security. More government regulations and controls became a normal part of American life. Unions were supported. Public works were initiated. The idea that "the business of America is business," as President Calvin Coolidge had once expressed as the then prevailing common sense in the 1920s, was rejected. The American welfare state was constructed. Along with such changes in policy, the arts and popular culture, social science, and a whole range of popular practices supported the changes and spirit of the "New Deal," followed by Truman's "Fair Deal," Kennedy's "New Frontier," and Johnson's "Great Society." Even Richard Nixon, a strong and partisan Republican, indicated his participation in the consensus when he famously declared in 1971, "We are all Keynesians now," indicating that he accepted the approach to the economy that justified the New Deal and continues to justify an active government role in the economy.

Associated with this political run was an account of the American Dream that emphasized the story of common people and was critical of corporate interests and the wealthy, perhaps most succinctly depicted in the films of Frank Capra, such as *It's* a *Wonderful Life*. The common sense was changed. The relationship between democracy and capitalism was reconfigured. The post Civil War, *laissez-faire* capitalist consensus was put to an end. Democratic state regulation, influence, and even control of the economy not only became acceptable in public policy and in the public mind. They were understood as being desirable.

Ronald Reagan's great achievement (given his political and cultural commitments), noted by Obama, was to overturn this common view. Reagan declared in his first inaugural address "government is not the solution to our problem, government is the problem" (Reagan, 1981). And he followed up with a series of policy decisions: attacking organized labor, weakening regulatory programs and agencies, and lowering taxes, particularly on the wealthy. He further intensified the Cold War, moving from peaceful coexistence to direct challenges to the "Evil Empire," and was equally resolute in the cultural wars, supporting "traditional values." He used his considerable rhetorical skills to create an unusual political coalition made up of anti-tax reformers, the so-called "supply-siders," religious-moral conservatives, the "moral majoritarians," and "neo-conservatives," the adamant cold warriors. The supporters of these distinct components of the "Reagan Revolution" disagreed on significant issues, in important ways, but the person of Reagan forged them together. Tradition, nativism, an untrammeled free market, and anti-Communism, with a touch of implicit racism (the so-called Southern strategy), were brought together in the political performance, in the acting abilities of Reagan, particularly on television.

And this was not all that different from what Roosevelt managed, keeping together the odd combination of Northern liberals and Southern racists, small farmers and trade unionists, that made up the New Deal coalition. Through fireside chats, his warm, reassuring radio performances, Roosevelt managed to keep together the disparate elements of the New Deal coalition, with an enduring legacy that lasted up to the Reagan years (see Wilentz, 2008). During the Reagan years, not only did government policy change. Wealth was celebrated and getting it was understood as an inherently ethical vocation. As the fictional tycoon, Gordon

Gekko, in the film *Wall Street* put it, "Greed is good." The story Americans told themselves about themselves changed, and this was linked with significant changes in American political practices. The approach to the state and capitalism was again reconfigured. Although the major public activities of the New Deal and of the Great Society of the sixties were not undone, the idea that the democratically elected government represented the common good as opposed to limited private interests was challenged. The public good came to be viewed as the summation of private interests. State activities, especially those directed to improve the situation of the less advantaged, came to be viewed as policies enacted for the "special interests" of the poor, the disabled, women, blacks, etc.

Obama understood these dynamics and has been dedicated to the project of turning things around, yet again. He has done this by adopting his party's positions, with minor variations on the themes of his fellow Democrats, but seeking to make these positions the new center, the new (bi-partisan) common sense. He is trying to achieve what Roosevelt and Reagan did, but with a difference; he is trying to do so as a centrist, not as a clear liberal or conservative. This nuanced position, a centrist with the goal to include in the center principles of the left, provoked his primary opponents, confused commentators and the general public, led people of the left and the center to support him to his electoral advantage, and has disoriented the general public in the first years of his presidency, hurting his popularity, too centrist for those on the left, too liberal for those in the center.

Nonetheless, beyond such tactical advantages and disadvantages, the project itself, in its distinctiveness, needs to be examined in analyzing the reinvention of political culture. The crucial starting point concerns the question of American identity which is the core of the Obama reinvention project. It has to do with addressing the fundamental enduring contradiction in American democracy, the contradiction of slavery and freedom, the problem of racism in a democratic society, what Gunnar Myrdal named "the American Dilemma" in his classic study (Myrdal, 1944).

76

Extending the American Dream by Addressing the American Dilemma

As he closed his acceptance of his party's nomination to be President, after advocating a long list of policy positions and after criticizing those of his Republican opponent, Obama depicted what he takes to be American strength and promise:

> This country of ours has more wealth than any nation, but that's not what makes us rich. We have the most powerful military on earth, but that's not what makes us strong. Our universities and our culture are the envy of the world, but that's not what keeps the world coming to our shores.

> Instead, it is that American spirit – that American promise – that pushes us forward even when the path is uncertain; that binds us together in spite of our differences; that makes us fix our eye not on what is seen, but what is unseen, that better place around the bend.

> That promise is our greatest inheritance. It's a promise I make to my daughters when I tuck them in at night, and a promise that you make to yours – a promise that has led immigrants to cross oceans and pioneers to travel west; a promise that led workers to picket lines, and women to reach for the ballot.

> And it is that promise that forty-five years ago today, brought Americans from every corner of this land to stand together on a mall in Washington, before Lincoln's Memorial, and hear a young preacher from Georgia speak of his dream.

> The men and women who gathered there could've heard many things. They could've heard words of anger and discord. They could've been told to succumb to the fear and frustration of so many dreams deferred.

> But what the people heard instead – people of every creed and color, from every walk of life – is that in America, our destiny is inextricably linked. That together, our dreams can be one.

> "We cannot walk alone," the preacher cried. "And as we walk, we must make the pledge that we shall always march ahead. We cannot turn back."

77

America, we cannot turn back. Not with so much work to be done. Not with so many children to educate, and so many veterans to care for. Not with an economy to fix and cities to rebuild and farms to save. Not with so many families to protect and so many lives to mend. America, we cannot turn back. We cannot walk alone. At this moment, in this election, we must pledge once more to march into the future. Let us keep that promise – that American promise – and in the words of Scripture hold firmly, without wavering, to the hope that we confess. (Obama, 2008)

As a biracial African American, he symbolically extended the American dream by embodying an overcoming of the American dilemma. As a gifted orator, he clearly envisioned something very different in the political culture. In the ages of Reagan and of Roosevelt, the problems of race were manipulated by some for political gain and were ignored by others for the same reasons.[29] Obama, in his person, in his identity, attacked this head on. And when he presented his vision of the common good, to be achieved by adopting the programs of his party, he envisioned a version of the American dream that is more inclusive. He was trying to expand the dream, speaking to the enduring common sense, and working to make it something else, working to address the great dilemma in the American experience emanating from the legacy of slavery.

In his acceptance of the Democratic Party's nomination, delivered on the forty-fifth anniversary of the March on Washington for Jobs and Freedom, the march during which Martin Luther King Jr. gave his famous "I have a dream" speech, Obama imagined a different America. He addressed the American dilemma in a subtle way. He vividly depicted an inclusive American dream. The imagery was active. Instead of commemorating King, which is the way that the march is conventionally remembered, Obama celebrated the people, in their great diversity, who actively took part in the march for justice. He did not even mention King's name, rather referring to "a young preacher from Georgia." Obama was making a broad appeal to all Americans to join him in his candidacy and his presidency, and he identified those who supported King in their diversity with those who will support him in his political work. By seeking to extend the dream by overcoming the dilemma, Obama was very much establishing a framework for working with King's legacy. By identifying the consequential work with the actions of his audience, he sought to make the work active. By presenting the bulk of his speech about, and by dedicating his candidacy with, the position of his party, he was trying to move the American common sense.

Obama's move to address the question of the American dilemma by expanding the imagination of the American dream is a key to the power of his politics, as candidate and as President. In his words, i.e., in the way he uses speech as an art form, Obama is working to retell the American story, certainly for his immediate political advantage, but more is involved. In fact through cultural creativity, he is attempting a reinvention of American political culture, moving common sense, informing new ways of developing our capacity for concerted action, and changing the ways the coercive powers of the state are legitimated. We will explore the significance of his artistry more fully below, but before we do so, we need to confront the reaction to his re-creation of the American story and to the other key dimension of his project of reinventing American political culture, concerning American understanding of the political economy.

The Reaction

The election of Obama has fundamentally changed the relationship between race and American democracy. The post-racial society has not become the existing reality, nor is it the case that race does not matter in American politics. Rather, it is that race matters in a different way.

I will show how this is working by contrasting key performances of Obama and former Vice Presidential candidate and Governor Sarah Palin, and by closely examining a racial media event, "Gates – Gate," concerning the arrest of Harvard Professor Henry Louis Gates Jr. and its aftermath.

Palin v. Obama

What does it mean to be an American? The contrasting visions presented by Obama and Palin reveal the new political cultural terrain. In Palin's speech at the Republican National Convention, she introduced herself and what she stood for:

> "We grow good people in our small towns, with honesty and sincerity and dignity," [quoting Westbrook Pegler]

> I grew up with those people. They're the ones who do some of the hardest work in America, who grow our food, and run our factories, and fight our wars. They love their country in good times and bad, and they're always proud of America.

> I had the privilege of living most of my life in a small town. I was just your average hockey mom and signed up for the PTA.

> I love those hockey moms. You know, they say the difference between a hockey mom and a pit bull? Lipstick.

> So I signed up for the PTA because I wanted to make my kids' public education even better. And when I ran for city council, I didn't need focus groups and voter profiles because I knew those voters, and I knew their families, too.

> Before I became governor of the great state of Alaska . . . I was mayor of my hometown. And since our opponents in this presidential election seem to look down on that experience, let me explain to them what the job involved.

> I guess – I guess a small-town mayor is sort of like a community organizer, except that you have actual responsibilities. (Palin, 2008)

Obama presents a clear alternative, as we have seen. His vision and identity have been extensively rendered, in many of his speeches and in his two books. He cut to the core in his victory speech in Chicago's Grant Park on Election Day, 2008. He stood there as the first African American elected President of the United States, and declared:

> If there is anyone out there who still doubts that America is a place where all things are possible; who still wonders if the dream of our

founders is alive in our time; who still questions the power of our democracy, tonight is your answer.

It's the answer told by lines that stretched around schools and churches in numbers this nation has never seen; by people who waited three hours and four hours, many for the very first time in their lives, because they believed that this time must be different; that their voice could be that difference.

It's the answer spoken by young and old, rich and poor, Democrat and Republican, black, white, Latino, Asian, Native American, gay, straight, disabled and not disabled – Americans who sent a message to the world that we have never been a collection of red states and blue states; we are, and always will be, the United States of America.

It's the answer that led those who have been told for so long by so many to be cynical, and fearful, and doubtful of what we can achieve to put their hands on the arc of history and bend it once more toward the hope of a better day.

It's been a long time coming, but tonight, because of what we did on this day, in this election, at this defining moment, change has come to America.

As he opened the celebration of his victory, Obama summarized what he thought his victory means for the American story and American identity. The contrast with Palin's presentation could not be more striking.

Palin celebrated the traditional values and the homogeneity of small-town America.[30] She tapped into a nostalgia for a rural American myth, building her speech around the words of Westbrook Pegler, an American racist of the mid twentieth century (see Frank, 2008). She returned to this theme during the campaign itself. In a speech she gave in Greensboro, North Carolina, she declared:

We believe that the best of America is in these small towns that we get to visit, and in these wonderful little pockets of what I call the real America, being here with all of you hard-working very patriotic, um, very, um, pro-America areas of this great nation. This is where we find the kindness and the goodness and the courage of everyday Americans. (see Leibovich, 2008).

Although it is not stated, this real America is homogeneous. It is not black, not foreign born, not the children of the foreign born, not gay, not Muslim, probably not Jewish.

Obama is clearly from the point of view of that world an out-sider. He has not looked at the past with nostalgia. Rather, he has searched the past for the future promise of inclusion. The American people of all races and creeds chose him to be their leader. This is a sea change, measured by its distance from the Palin ideal.

America is the place that is open, where a man of African and Muslim, as well as Christian and agnostic, ancestry became the leader of the country. That this could and did happen re-defines what the nation is. This made Obama not only popular, as meas-ured by the election results, specifically among all groups who have been excluded from full participation in the American dream, or feel so excluded: blacks and browns, Latinos and Asians, Jews and Muslims, and youth and women.[31] It also has made him popular around the globe: more popular in many nations than their own leaders, a "brand" that many up-and-coming politicians seek to be associated with (Wong, 2009). He has presented a very attractive American face to the world.

But back home, there have been problems with this. It appeared first during the campaign when Obama's immense popularity in Europe, revealed in the enthusiastic Berlin rally of hundreds of thousands of people, seemed to hurt his election prospects rather than enhance them (Armbruster, 2008). And it has reappeared repeatedly during his presidency when controversies over specific policy actions, from the stimulus package to health care have been interpreted as fundamentally undermining the social order. Obama's identity as someone who personifies the previously excluded has been difficult to take for many of those who are attached to the old order of things. His practical policies have been seen as being foreign, not truly American (D'Souza, 2010).

This was most dramatically expressed in the approach of talk show ideologues and echoed among members of their audience. Glenn Beck, who became the Counter-Revolutionary-in-Chief, on reparations and health care: "Barack Obama is setting up universal health care, universal college, green jobs as stealth reparations. That way the victim status is maintained. And he also brings back-door reparations" (Beck, 2009). His logic is inventive. For a long time, there has been an understanding among Democratic politicians, starting with Bill Clinton, that the way to address the problems of race and still maintain broad support for the policies is to address the problems of class. Help the poor and you will help African Americans and other disadvantaged groups, because they are disproportionately poor. This position builds upon the sociology and public policy advice of William Julius Wilson (Wilson, 1971, 2001). Beck sees this as a kind of hidden reparations, rather than a project for social justice.

And, as Clarence Page, the *Chicago Tribune* columnist, observed, "Beck is not alone in his twisted logic. Rush Limbaugh, the Big Kahuna of conservative radio talkers, declared in a June broadcast that Obama's 'entire economic program is reparations,' although Limbaugh did not explain why he thinks that way. The mere mention of the R-word is enough in Limbaugh's logic to condemn Obama's 'wealth redistribution'."

Page continues to argue that this has a significant result, using the example of a disabled sheet-rock installer, Richie Drake from Virginia, as an indication that this kind of race baiting works. Drake, unemployed and with children on Medicaid, said to a radio reporter about Obama's reforms, "Minorities are going to get more attention than the whites and stuff like that [. . .] That's the way I take it from what the news was talking about" (Page, 2009).

Significant change has been initiated, and there has been resistance. Both the change and its connection to the power of the state, and the resistance and its connection to opposition media and social movements,[32] organized and spontaneous, indicate a transformation of American political culture. The relationships between racist and anti-racist culture and democratic power have changed, as many problems persist or appear in new forms.

Gates-Gate

Racism's persistence and change in American political culture are revealed in periodic explosions of racial controversy. From decisions about affirmative action, to the killing and brutalization of innocents, from Emmett Till to Abner Louima, to the prosecution of a black media celebrity charged and convicted of killing his white wife, i.e., the strange case of O.J. Simpson, the character of racism is clearly revealed (see Pollack and Metress, 2008; Chan, 2007; Schuetz and Lilly, 1999). These events may not be at the core of the problem of racism. That is manifested more in the daily struggles and interactions of ordinary people, beyond the public eye, as they get on with their lives. But the events, media events, permit the symbolic enactment of American moral codes about race (Dayan and Katz, 1992; Wagner-Pacifici, 2010).

Blacks and whites perceived the OJ trial and acquittal differently. In and of itself this would appear to be a trivial matter. It took on great significance because it revealed how separately and differently blacks and whites live and perceive themselves and each other in America. Distinctions, differences and commonalities about race were revealed.[33] With an African American President, such a case, which inevitably appears periodically in American life, has taken on a new dimension. The head of state, the central symbol of authority in the society, is now black, and this necessarily has meaning. The first case in point in the course of the Obama presidency is "Gates-gate," a socio-political drama in three parts.

Part 1: A local affair in Cambridge, Massachusetts. Henry Louis Gates Jr. returned from a trip to China, ironically working on a television documentary on the heterogeneous racial, ethnic, and national genealogy of Americans.[34] When he and his driver were trying to open his front door, finding that it was jammed, a neighbor thinking that they might be burglars called the police. The police investigation led to the arrest of Gates in his own home, with Gates asserting racial profiling, and with Sgt. James Crowley, the arresting officer, charging Gates with disorderly conduct. The charges were subsequently dropped (Goodnough, 2009).

The characters in the affair are noteworthy. Gates is a distinguished professor at Harvard, a renowned scholar and public intellectual.[35] As a student of African American culture, he is careful and sober, not a flaming radical. Crowley, ironically, is a police academy expert on racial profiling, teaching a course on the subject at the Lowell Police Academy. And in many ways the two are on the same side of the cultural wars. Both Gates and Crowley have cooperated with the Simon Wiesenthal Center, Crowley having participated in a three-day workshop on Racial Profiling at the Simon Wiesenthal Center's Museum of Tolerance in Los Angeles in 2007, Gates delivering the Center's Third Annual "State of Antisemitism" Lecture in New York in 1994 (Simon Wiesenthal Center, 2009). These were odd antagonists in what turned out to be a major national affair.

Part 2: The local becomes national. The event was first covered by *The Harvard Crimson*, but given Gates's prominence, and the irony that he was apparently arrested for breaking into his own home, it became a national story, covered by the national media. As such affairs go, it followed the conventional black and white script. There were those who clearly saw the ugly face of racism pure and simple, and there were those who sided with the cop and stressed the importance of maintaining and respecting law and order. The usual suspects, provocateurs of the left and right, played starring roles in the performance: Reverend Al Sharpton, Rush Limbaugh, et al. (Breitbart, 2009). And then many others chimed in, with varying degrees of insightfulness. Professional observers of the problem of racial profiling noted that bias is often not conscious. It emerges from psychological perceptions of the other, and in a society with a long history of racism, these perceptions do not change quickly or easily. Accepted prevailing practices may be fashioned to overcome this problem, but they do not necessarily succeed (*New York Times*, 2009). It was observed that "a proud cop" met "an arrogant professor," but if the professor had been white, an arrest would not have resulted (Fish, 2009). Further, a close look at the case as it developed in its details revealed both that race mattered in its classic form (Herbert, 2009), and that the real problems are political correctness and reverse racism (Breibart, 2009).

Part 3: The national became explicitly political when Obama weighed in. His comment on the Gates arrest came at the end of a long and detailed news conference on health-care reform. Asked what he thought about the arrest, the *New York Times* reported that:

> Mr. Obama took it [the question] head on, noting that "I may be a little biased" because he is friends with Mr. Gates but condemning the police in Cambridge, Mass.

> He said: "I think it's fair to say, No. 1, any of us would be pretty angry. No. 2, the Cambridge police acted stupidly in arresting somebody when there was already proof that they were in their own home. And No. 3, what I think we know separate and apart from this incident is there is a long history in this country of African-Americans and Latinos being stopped by police disproportionately. That's just a fact." (Baker, Cooper, and Nagourney, 2009)

Obama admitted that he did not know all the facts in the case and he explicitly did not accuse anyone of racial bias, but the implication was there for all to comment on, and they did.

The debate intensified. It started with the arrest and was a continuation of an ongoing theme: dealing with the problems of race in America, including the very different perceptions of the problem across the population. Those with clear positions presented them forcefully, and they were joined by the beltway pundits who commented on the practical implications of the response, without much reference to the normative issues involved (Newman, 2009). Obama backtracked, recognizing that he had inflamed the situation by calling the Cambridge police actions stupid, and he invited Crowley and Gates for a beer at the White House to diffuse the situation, which it did (Cooper and Goodnough, 2009). Another moment in the continuing struggle to talk about the problems of race and American democracy passed. But this one was different, having to do with the fundamental issue of political culture: the relationship between culture and power. Things were turned around, a revolution of sorts was apparent.

This was the first race media event with an African American

President, posing problems for the media, for Obama, and for his critics. Commentators noted that Obama made a big mistake by offering his opinion on the matter, as one put it, speaking more as a person than as a President (Parker, 2009). Among these observers, there seemed to be a general consensus that Obama's statement was a mistake. His intervention undermined his attempts to enact health-care reform. He was getting involved with a local issue, best left alone by the head of state. He got involved even as he admitted to not having all the facts at his disposal. Obama and his advisors did have second thoughts about what he said. He appeared unannounced at a White House press briefing indicating regret for "ratcheting it up" the controversy (Baker and Cooper, 2009). Yet, it seems to me that he had no choice but to get involved. He was asked a direct question at a press conference. Not to respond with a direct answer would have appeared as calculating, open to a range of undesirable interpretations. And no response also would have been understood as a response. Perhaps political pundits, the professional insiders and the commentators, would have approved of the pragmatism, applauding his decision to stay on the central message of the conference, the need for health-care reform. But in the long run, beyond such media commentary, Obama would have been criticized for compromising fundamental principle. An African American leader who refuses to address racial controversy would not appear as principled.

Much was made of the forcefulness of Obama's statement, but in fact it was circumspect. He indicated a suspicion that the event was part of the long story of racism, but he did not criticize it as such. He called the action stupid, but he did not condemn it as a moral outrage.

A President who was not African American would not have been asked about the Gates affair. An African American President once asked about the affair had to answer. Staying within his fundamental project of expanding the American dream by addressing the American dilemma, the President had to be open and clear about his position, while recognizing the complexities.

And crucially, this was the voice of official power, a fundamental change in the political culture. Those who dissented from his vision attacked his intervention. Those focused on the politics of the news cycle questioned its wisdom. But racial politics have been thus transformed. The terrain has been reordered. Race and racial conflict are still very much a part of the American political scene, but how they are manifested has changed radically.

Democracy and Capitalism: The Market Fundamentalists' Last Stand?

The second primary way that Barack Obama sought to change common sense concerned the relationship between democracy and capitalism. He sought to qualify Reagan's fundamental principle that government is not the answer to our problems – it is the problem, which has been broadly accepted by the population. When Clinton (1996) in his Inaugural Address in 1996 declared that "the era of big government was over," this was roughly equivalent to the time that Nixon asserted that we are all Keynesians now. Obama wanted to change this. Not in the sense that he wanted to usher in a new era of big government, but in that he perceived that there needed to be a correction in policy, a change in common sense. His attempt to change the common sense of Reaganism has been a struggle.

There was great urgency about these matters even before Obama took office. An irony is that even as major government intervention was broadly understood as being necessary by policy makers across the political spectrum, the cultural support for such actions lagged. Bush and the Republicans retreated from their asserted hands off the economy position, but there was not broad understanding concerning these changed policies. Reinventing or at least redirecting the political culture was the challenge that was particularly difficult. The problem has deep historical roots. The resistance to more government action in economic affairs is very much tied to the major ideological battle of the twentieth century, and the way that battle has been understood across the political spectrum after the collapse of Communism.

In the twentieth century, the question of the relationship

between capitalism and democracy was indeed addressed ideologically, and the ideologies prevailed through geo-politics. On the left, in the political east, among socialists, capitalism was seen to be the enemy of democracy. It created an unequal society, a class society, and this was seen as being fundamentally at odds with the requirements of democracy and equal democratic participation of all citizens. On the right and the center, in the west, among liberals and conservatives, the free market was understood as a precondition for the free politics that democracy required. Monopolized economic control, state control of the economy, was understood to lead to monopolized political control.

As we observed in chapter 2, these two competing ideological positions were tested with the collapse of Communism. It became more difficult to express with certainty the anti-capitalist position for many on the left. There was a growing pragmatic attitude. The market was no longer demonized. State intervention in the economy was no longer understood as being the solution of first resort to solve societal problems.

On the right, on the other hand, the certainty of market fundamentalists has continued, even when there has been strong evidence that the market is not the answer to all problems. The pressing need to address the problems of the world financial crisis and the great recession and the election of Obama indicated a shift away from this fundamentalism. But with the twists and turns of the recovery and the sustained attempt by the Obama administration to enact reforms addressing energy independence and environmental degradation, problems of education and health-care reform, there has been a kind of last stand of market fundamentalists, revealed in the elections of 2010. There has been opposition not only to specific policies, but there has also been fundamental opposition based on the notion that the market is the best solution to all problems. This has been most evident in the debate about health-care reform, which has been in important ways really a debate about the relationship between capitalism and democracy. Common sense has been the issue. The strong protests against reform have been less about the specifics of the way health insurance is organized and delivered, more about what the role of the state should be.

As a world financial collapse appeared to be an imminent reality, reasonable Republicans and Democrats worked together to develop a rescue plan. Even Senators McCain and Obama, the Republican and Democratic candidates for the President of the United States, did so. The leadership in this development shifted after the election, from the Bush team to the Obama team, but the appreciation of a pressing economic crisis resulted in a rational bipartisan public policy. It succeeded. There were disagreements about details, but informed leadership, on the left and the right, understood the necessity of government action, and the necessary action was taken. But almost immediately "the give-away" was condemned by Obama's opposition, and this, along with opposition to a stimulus package, set the stage for the partisan struggle that greeted the Obama administration. The Republicans, with only a few exceptions, rejected just about all of the new administration's initiatives. In the case of the economic policies, the opposition was cast in clear ideological terms: market – good, government – bad. They reverted to their pre-crisis position, which was an extension of a long-established one.

The general contours of the opposition were revealed in town hall meetings, such as the one reported by the *New York Times*, between Senator Arlen Specter of Pennsylvania and his constituents (Urbina and Seelye, 2009). Such town hall meetings, the progress of which was dominated by the Tea Party Movement, which I will analyze below, generated more heat than light on the specific issues involved. The meetings were not occasions of rational debate and deliberation on specific issues, but they did reveal the resistance to the reinvention of American political culture, the changing relationship between power and the cultural orientations that support power. Carolyn Doric in the heat of the confrontation with Senator Specter underlined the crucial issue, "political power and the means to regain political power." The repeated calls "to take the country back" in the town hall meetings, the questioning of Obama's citizenship and legitimacy, against the factual evidence that he was born in the United States, revealed a broad sentiment that power had been wrested away from its right-ful carriers. Issues of the political economy and political identity were merged. As the right wing media performers led this opposi-tion, the Republican Party representatives and leaders, with few exceptions, followed (Herszenhorn, 2010). A first principle of these "rightful carriers" was that government is the problem, not the solution, that capitalism should be unfettered. But implied in the notion of taking our country back is the idea of "them and us," us of the real America, versus them, those who have taken our country away from us. Less provocatively put: two oppos-ing views of America are in conflict, and race and other social differences are involved. Also notable was the slippage between strong ideological opposition to an active government role to wild attacks upon Barack Obama, the person and his individual story.

The opposition was often presented in the most extreme tones. Obama was regularly condemned for being a socialist and a fascist. His legitimacy as President of the United States was questioned by a majority of Republicans polled,[36] and provoked the so-called "birthers movement" which claimed that he was not a citizen because he was not born in the United States. The Republican rank and file and leadership responded to him as a radical, and so did the 24/7 opposition media apparatus – Fox News and "con-servative" (right wing) talk radio. This was all part of the same ideological package. Obama was understood as challenging the fundamental rules of the game, and he was attacked for this.

Conservative Republicans viewed Obama through a sharply focused ideological lens. As reported by *On the Hill*:

An overwhelming 91 percent of the conservative Republican base label President Obama a socialist, Marxist, communist, or fascist, according to a new online poll conducted on a conservative website.

Some 1,848 self-identified conservatives, 46 percent label Obama "socialist," 24 percent as "Marxist," 11 percent as "communist," and 10 percent as "fascist."

Only 7 percent responding to the poll on the ConservativeHQ. com website consider the president to be a liberal (5 percent), or a progressive (2 percent). The poll was conducted May 12 through 19, according to an announcement of the poll results.

The poll results come amidst official efforts by the Republican National Committee to label Democrats as the "Democrat Socialist Party." "While this is not a scientific poll of conservatives, it is a meaningful indicator that most conservatives (the GOP base) see Obama as a dangerous radical," says Richard Viguerie, chairman of ConservativeHQ.com and a longtime conservative author and activist. "Rather than Americans coming together as a result of the election, it appears that America is becoming much more polarized.

"Because so many conservatives see President Obama as a radical leftist, Republican politicians will be under pressure to step up their criticism of President Obama and the Democrats who are closely cooperating with him," says Viguerie, author of *Conservatives Betrayed: How George W. Bush and Other Big Government Republicans Hijacked the Conservative Cause.*

The strong perception among conservatives likely will make Obama's outreach to the GOP for bipartisanship more difficult. "It will also make compromise more difficult for GOP officials. Any Republican who wants to be a national leader will feel obligated to view Obama as the vast majority of the GOP base sees him," says Viguerie, credited as a pioneer of political direct mail. (On the Hill, 2009)

Thus, the head of the Republican Party, Michael Steele, in the middle of a serious discussion about health reform gave what he admitted was a political speech to the National Press Club. He labeled the various plans for health-care reform coming out of Congress as "socialist" and agreed with Senator Jim DeMint's assessment that health-care reform was Obama's Waterloo (Stein, 2009). The ideological equivalent of war was declared.

The Politics of Small Things

The struggle for reinvention went beyond changes in policy concerning the relationship between capitalism and democracy and the redefinitions of American identity by a gifted orator-political leader and his opponents. The way the campaign was practiced, the way people participated, was significant. This mode of re-invention, ironically, Obama and his critics shared: in the campaign for Obama's nomination and election and in the formation and actions of the Tea Party. Each is an example of the politics of small things, when people meet each other, talk, and act in each others' presence, develop a capacity to act on the basis of shared principles, and, in the process, create power (Goldfarb, 2006). The way they do this is as significant as the results it yields both in the case of the Obama project to reinvent American political culture, and the Tea Party resistance.

The Obama Campaign

What Obama's supporters did was probably as important as what he said. Hannah Arendt tells us that in politics the means are the ends (see "Truth and Politics" in Arendt, 1961). This was strikingly the case in the Obama campaign. The configuration of his policy positions and his redefinition of the political culture were enacted by those engaged in the campaign. There was a practical foundation, a micro infrastructure, to the Obama candidacy, and this became a foundation of his presidency. It was observable on the web and in the everyday life of the campaign. It was the result of independent social interaction. The cultural vision of a political leader was linked with the political practices of his supporters.

Most noteworthy was how the campaign built upon the accomplishments of the Dean campaign that preceded it. The point is not that Obama, and Dean before him, successfully used the internet to raise funds and mobilize support for their campaigns. Rather, it is the other way around: the campaign formed around a social movement and the social movement formed around the campaigns, facilitated by web interactions, and these interactions defined the broad political significance of the campaign. There was an added level of reflectivity to the Obama campaign. This configuration is also observable in the Tea Party Movement. Participation is a key to avoiding the underside of democracy as

Tocqueville understood it. Such participation is now observable across the political spectrum.

The participation among Obama's supporters was not only instrumental and explicitly political; also involved were the pleasures of "sociation," as Georg Simmel understood this (Levine, 1972). People met each other on and off the web and discussed the campaign. Think of café interactions and political hangouts and then log onto youtube.com. Note that there were 775 videos, at the height of the campaign in March, 2008, about Obama. These were quite varied, including formal speeches given at critical moments of the campaign: Obama's announcement of his candidacy in Springfield, his Jefferson-Jackson Speech in Iowa, "the defining moment of the campaign" (Brooks, 2008), his eloquent speeches following Primary victories and defeats, and, of course, his speech on race.[37] There were also briefer and lighter videos: short campaign ads, videos of engaged voters on the campaign trail expressing their support, and, very significantly, creative uploads, including the silly "The Obama Girl," and the engaging "Yes We Can" videos. The latter is a creative singalong with a portion of Obama's New Hampshire concession speech: classical oration meets pop music. Thousands of people commented on these, arguing political points, making jokes, attacking each other. This was a public space for people to meet each other and exchange views, often not of a very serious nature. Again, think of café conversations and the corner bar, not the literary public sphere of Habermas.

Nonetheless, this is a public space with clear political potential (Gutman and Goldfarb, 2010). The "Yes We Can" video has a running discussion following it. The song was released on February 2, 2008, and after which people used its discussion thread to debate the campaign. By March 5, 2008, at 5:30 p.m., as I looked at this closely, there had been 52,856 comments. People listened to and watched the video and debated the fate of the campaign, as the campaign unfolded. Of course, this was only one place, and not a very serious one, where such discussion took place.

For the more focused and instrumental, there were the more

directed sites of the campaign and supporting websites, such as moveon.org. For those who wished more personalized interactions associated with the Obama candidacy, there were the connections made through social networking sites, such as facebook.com and myspace.com. All of this added up to a rich network of social interactions, from the most instrumental to the most entertaining. It allowed people to easily find each other, speak to each other and do things together, *small things* that add up. Involved was the kind of political power, as analyzed in chapter 1, which Arendt highlighted.

In the actual campaign, people moved back and forth between the virtual and the embodied, between entertaining and sober debate, and, for those who sought it, on to serious political engagement. The most evident engagement was revealed in fund-raising. The capacity to raise money was astounding, with tremendous political results. The conventional means of fundrais-ing and paying for a campaign have been overwhelmed by the interactive politics of the web. But the power of the new politics went far beyond this.

People were organized and enlisted in the campaign through a combination of face-to-face interaction, group emailing, mes-sages on social networking sites, and text messaging. This is one of the ways that the Obama campaign distinguished itself from the Dean campaign, apart from the crucial differences between these two political leaders. The Obama campaign worked with the new forms of interaction, enlisted people through them, as people formed their own social circles. There was active interac-tion among supporters, as there was the attempt to interact and lead these supporters on the part of the campaign leadership. In this way, Obama consistently won in caucus contests. Apart from his popularity in these states, this speaks well to the organizational prowess of his campaign. Decisive in the caucuses, it was also a key to Primary elections and the general election as well. People were brought together and found each other. They were engaged by the leadership, and they planned and coordinated their local strategies for getting out the vote. They were aided by campaign officials, but did much of the work on their own.

The level of participation in the campaign and the degree of enthusiasm of the Obama supporters indicated significant change in the political culture. More people participated (as measured by voter turnout), and they developed together new ways of participating, on the web and in embodied interactions. After years of increased voter apathy, negative media campaigns, and broad cynicism, principled engagement was broadly observable. Tocqueville believed that American broad voluntary participation in political and non-political associations would counter the atomizing tendencies of democratic society, and that Americans would thus avoid "the despotism that democratic nations have to fear" (2000: 661–5). Recent experience suggests that this despotism, the despotism suffered by an enervated population in a mass society, is very much a clear and present danger in American society. This is the concern of the neo-Tocquevillians, the followers of Robert Putnam (Putnam, 2000). Yet, not only in the Obama campaign but also in the opposition to the Obama presidency, there are new developments that suggest that this concern may be exaggerated, or more precisely to the degree to which it was on the mark, the problem has been successfully addressed. This is especially clear when we examine the other side of the political spectrum and see a similar development of extensive and intensive participation.

The Tea Party

Politics is as much about the means of political action as its ends. And herein lies a clear transformation in American political culture. People actively participated in inventive new ways. Obama supporters met each other on web logs of the anti-war, anti-Bush left, the Obama campaign and the Democratic Party. We met each other in virtual and face-to-face interactions. We developed a capacity to act in concert and we overwhelmed the political opposition. Now, in opposition to Obama, the same pattern is observable. It is an impressive manifestation of a heightened popular involvement in political life. This too is part of the reinvention of a political culture. American politics now, insomuch as they are about the kind of power Arendt highlighted, have been fundamentally changed.

During the struggle to enact health-care reform in the first year of the Obama administration, the summer recess of Congress led to a social movement contest. Members of Congress returned to their states and districts and held open forum with their constituents. The town hall meetings became battlegrounds over common sense. The supporters of the reforms, including President Obama, attempted to explain their reform ideas and to defend themselves against strong dissent. There was a sense among the supporters that those who had interest in the status quo, specifically the insurance industry, those who defeated every attempt at health-care reform in the last seventy years, were responsible for organizing the dissenters at the town hall meetings. Their claim was that this was not a grassroots movement but "Astroturf," an artificial grassroots movement. But the dissenters and their supporters, including most Republicans in Congress, recognized the protests as a genuine expression of deep public concern specifically about health-care reform and more generally about an overreaching big government. The political culture changed: not with a victory of the opponents of market fundamentalism, but with the real struggle over the issue of the relationship between democracy and capitalism, democracy and the market.

The resistance borrowed a great deal from the mobilization of the Obama campaign. The critics of Obama used the pending health-care legislation during the summer recess of Congress as the occasion to express and mobilize their opposition to Obama's presidency. The proximate cause was the health-care initiative. But clearly much more was involved. This is apparent both by the performances at the town hall meetings and in the virtual interactions on the various websites and television and radio programs.[38]

On the programs and through these websites, market fundamentalists have promoted their protests, discussed the issues involved, and planned tactics and strategies. The leadership of the movement self-consciously tried to reproduce the methods of the Obama campaign and the anti-war movement. Indeed they made a point of discussing how they used the ideas of the radical activist, Saul Alinsky, ideas which guided Barack Obama's community organizing in the late 1980s. "What's sauce for the goose is sauce for the gander," declared Dick Armey, the former House Minority Whip and a major Obama opponent. "What I think of Alinsky is that he was very good at what he did but what he did was not good" (Luce and Ulmer, 2009). Armey was interested in using Alinsky's tactics for ends which were quite opposed to those of Alinsky and Obama.

In the town hall meetings, it became standard fare to repeat a number of clearly enumerated talking points, following the guidance of a carefully organized national movement. "Freedom Works," Dick Armey's significant web base, presented pointed explanations for opposition to the health-care reform and cap and trade reforms, an "August Recess Action Kit," and a guide for finding local town hall meetings around the country. They presented on their website materials to print and share with fellow activists. "Health Care Petitions," "ObamaCare Insurance Cards," a "9/12 Invitation Flyer" (for a mass demonstration against Obama's policies on that date), "an ObamaCare Translator – [to] cut through the spin," and a critical account of "How Many Are Really Uninsured?" were all included.[39] People responded to this and other organizing efforts.

There were planned disruptions of the meetings, meant to interfere with deliberate questions from constituents and answers from members of Congress. Activists went to the meetings armed with protest posters distributed for local gatherings through national campaigns. Shouting protesters demonstrated outside the President's town hall meetings. Videos were made of the meetings and were uploaded on movement websites and youtube.com. All of this has been reported by and supported on media outlets that are sympathetic to the cause of opposing Obama, specifically Fox News and Foxnews.com.

Much of the activity and the reports were very dramatic, town hall protesters shouting at members of Congress, about Obama and the Nazis and the like, but they included as well calm, ordinary people deeply concerned by the issues. As the *New York Times* reported: "The cameras may linger on those at the extremes, but it is the parade of respectful questioners, those expressing discomfiting fears and legitimate concerns, that may ultimately have more impact" (Sack, 2009). In this *Times* report on the movement, a report that highlighted the deep-felt concerns of town hall protester, Bob Collier of Montezuma, Georgia, though, indicated that such calm protestors still reverted to the simplifications of sound-bite talk TV and radio. The reporter, Kevin Sack, did not emphasize this, but his report revealed it. "This is about the future of our country as we know it," Collier declared to Sack, "and may mean the end of our country as we know it." Pointing to the cause: "Here comes this new guy in town, and he wants to centralize everything. He wants to take over the car companies. He wants to take over the banks. Now he wants to take over health care. It's a power grab, and if he gets this, there's no turning it around." On the health-care bill and Obama's assurance that the elderly will not have to wait in line behind those with longer life expectancies, Collier declared: "I don't trust him on that ... I think you're going to have all the efficiency of the post office with the compassion of the IRS" (a stock line of the opposition). Collier worries that tax dollars will go to "lazy and irresponsible people who play the system." But he is energized and feels connected as a result of attending a town hall meeting, "You don't know what you're getting when you send an email to those guys," he said. "You don't know what you're getting when you call one of their people. But when you can talk to him face to face like that, it's a great opportunity." Many people independently became engaged, some, like Collier, for the first time in their lives.

This is the Tea Party Movement, an instance of "the politics of small things," a version on the right. I am not a supporter of the aims of this movement, as I was of the Obama campaign and the anti-war movement, and earlier of the democratic opposition in the former Soviet bloc. In those instances of "the politics of small things," I was very much both a participant and an observer. But even though I am not so involved or supportive of this new instance of the politics of small things, I recognize it for what it is. People have been meeting each other, sharing opinions, discussing strategies, coordinating tactics, and becoming clearly visible to each other and to outside observers. Power has been created in these interactions. This cannot be artificially manufactured. It would not exist unless people willingly and actively took part. The success of this depended upon active participants interacting with others and bringing themselves along. Even if there are powerful forces behind this movement, its political power is primarily generated by people acting in concert, as they take part in the town hall meetings, in demonstrations, such as the one organized for September 12, 2009 in Washington, and through their interactions with each other, especially as these interactions become visible through various media forms. They became a significant part of the political landscape, demanding attention, and this has influenced public life. Thus, the resistance to Obama's changes in public policies has been significant, while it is also confirming the changes of greater citizenship participation that was one of the hallmarks of his campaign.

Media and Reinvention

While Obama and his opponents both use the politics of small things in opposition to each other, it is important to note that the way they operate in the media environment is quite different. Obama affirms cultural traditions and received notions of excellence, trying to find a place for conventional rhetoric. He is forging a media strategy beyond sound bytes, while his opponents are sound-bite masters, innovatively developing new ways to use radio and cable TV to persuade. While media performances empower in both cases, the way they empower is quite different.

The success of Obama's media performance is ironic. He has classical rhetorical skills. These are not particularly well suited to broadcast television. His speeches are most convincing in their entirety.[40] The rhythms of his words, sentences, and paragraphs are carefully crafted and delivered, revealing a coherent vision of the public good and the way he, along with his listeners, can contribute to it. He is a superior orator when one listens to his speeches from beginning to end and compares them to those of his opponents. But when the speeches are reduced to sound bytes, as most people hear them, he and his opponents are not very different. He is not all that much more convincing.

Joshua Meyrowitz (1986), combining the insights of Erving Goffman and Marshall McLuhan, in *No Sense of Place,* suggests why such is the case. As we view the television, the different experiences of gender, race, age, and authority are breaking down. In our viewing, we are all in the same place, and we cannot distinguish easily the proprieties of place or status (Krabel, 2002). Important distinctions have been undermined, not the least of which are the distinctions between the public and the private, and the language styles of both. Grand eloquence, Meyrowitz maintains, thinking specifically about Ronald Reagan when he made these observations, is a thing of the past. "The great communicator" had a sunny, everyday, intimate voice. It convinced, transforming the form of political eloquence (Jamieson, 1988).

Yet, with a very different voice, more formal and precise, more traditional, Obama has moved people, working the media to his advantage. This suggests a new form of successful media politics, media politics beyond sound bytes. His is a classical eloquence facilitated by the web going against the media grain of the television. Interested in hearing a speech in its entirety? Go to the web, see and hear it, and discuss it with your fellow citizens.

Media focus, not media bias, has become a central issue, and the politics of media now is significantly about sustaining the focus. A close, tight focus, the presentation of video clips and sound bytes, in the mode of network television and its cable variants, fosters narrow political understanding and is easily susceptible to manipulation,[41] while more distant focus and deliberate consideration reveal political realities that are often ignored. Obama has sustained distance and deliberation to his great advantage during his campaign, but has struggled to do so as President. He has used the quality of his rhetoric to move the public. Elegance of expression has answered various forms of populist appeals throughout the campaign and during his presidency.

The presidential campaign on a day-to-day basis, in tight focus, seemed to progress as campaigns have in the recent past.

Competing sound bites and "got-ya" journalism, facilitated by the ubiquitous presence of blogging reporters, dominated the media reporting. High points were Bill Clinton's comparison of Obama's victory in the South Carolina Primary with Jesse Jackson's earlier victories in that state, Obama's remarks about the white working class clinging to their guns and religion, and John McCain maintaining that the fundamentals of the economy are strong.[42] These things, for better and worse, mattered.

But Obama worked to present a different political dimension, with a distant focus, revealed in his speeches and their progression. Indeed, at critical moments in his run for the presidency, Obama moved the public through carefully crafted and delivered speeches, the most remarkable case in point being his Philadelphia "Race Speech."[43] As he has made important substantive arguments, he has worked against the previously existing grain of media politics. He offered a more sober and substantive politics in form and content, which became apparent in his speeches as they individually addressed particular problems and challenges, and as they all have been connected.

There is a sense in which the Obama campaign and his presidency present refutations of Tocqueville's judgments about the relationship between democracy and culture. He believed that the need for hierarchical judgment in culture was fundamentally at odds with the egalitarian ethos of democracy. Works of art, literature, music, and also history and political rhetoric would appeal to the greatest number, substituting quantity for quality, requiring little work for understanding and appreciation. Tocqueville's position summarizes, echoes, and anticipates elitist criticism of American culture. Yet, he was an elitist with an important difference, because he posited a tension between quality and quantity, refinement and popularity, leading to results that he himself did not anticipate.

In many of the great works of American culture, and democratic culture more generally, this tension yields new creativity and vitality, as has already been explored in chapter 1. In Obama's speech, this tension raises the level of political discourse. He has told the story of America to America in his many speeches. He responds, as politicians must, to immediate circumstances. But his responses add up. Responding to the long history of America, Obama places the immediate problems as a part of that long history, revealing his reinvention project.[44]

His Republican and Tea Party opposition has not responded in kind, probably because it could not. The counter-revolution is not only about matters of substance, public policy, and political vision. It is also about media tactics that have attacked not only Obama's substantive positions, but also the quality of his public persuasion. He has attempted to bring people together, Republicans and Democrats, to discuss pressing issues of our times, i.e., this is the way he presents his positions. They have responded with provocative sound bites, with uncertain relationships with factual reality, e.g., death panels (Palin) which would pull the plug on grandma (Senator Grassley) (see Rutenberg and Calmes, 2008; Zeleny, 2009). He would like to have serious debate about the competing merits of various reforms, concerning such issues as health care, climate change, financial overhaul, and immigration, while they have engaged in hyperbolic polemics, with talk radio and TV hosts seeming to set the agenda.

Indeed, it is noteworthy that many of those who did join the Tea Party were people who came to know the issues involved and became active through the cable television network, Fox News, and its various reporters and commentators. While there has been significant web activity facilitating this opposition, of the sort we have just observed, Fox News, along with talk radio of Rush Limbaugh et al., played a central role in this movement.[45] The upcoming meetings and demonstrations were announced on Fox. Then Fox would thoroughly report on the events. The network helped organize the events, and their coverage confirmed their importance. This was unprecedented in American political and media history. The counter-revolution did not only have key substantive themes. It also had a set of media relationships that empowered the counter-revolutionaries.

Fox News is not just biased. It is a political mobilization machine, shaping the political landscape. It has developed a truly innovative media form, particularly for television. It purports to present news, but actually it is in the business of political mobilization.

In the case of the Tea Party protests, this is most clearly the case. Fox news commentator, Glenn Beck, announced a mass demonstration, the 9/12 rally. On the Fox News programs and discussion shows, the developments leading up to the demonstration were reported, and their significance was discussed. Together with Beck's agitation for the event, these reports and discussions bring the planned event to the attention of a large audience. Even if the event was initially the result of grassroots organization, as were the Tea Party protests called for "tax day," April 15, 2009, the attention of the public to the event far exceeded the intentions of its original planners and their capacity to mobilize the population as a result of Fox's reporting. Then the event happened and Fox was there giving it full coverage. It was their major event of the day, the story that was given wall-to-wall coverage, while the other news sources tended to report it as one story among many. The fact that only Fox "properly" reported on the event was said to reveal the bias of the "lame stream media," to use the language of the American media critic and Fox commentator, Sarah Palin. The format applies to major happenings, but also to the trivial, from the Islamic bias of textbooks in Texas, to the booing of Palin's daughter Bristol on "Dancing with the Stars." Fox is not just biased as it reports the news. It produces the news from beginning to end. There is nothing like it on the left side of the political spectrum.

Conclusion

I have been describing Obama's project to reinvent American political culture as a revolution, suggesting that his opponents' resistance is a counter-revolution. The reinvention and its opposition is a revolution in the sense of Hannah Arendt. There is a project to turn things around, and bring something new into the world, and there has been inventive resistance to this turning, also bringing something new into the world.

As Obama has worked to transform the center of American political life, his opponents have pushed back. In some ways, this is just a matter of competing policy positions, for or against one program or another: on health care, climate change, financial regulation, etc. But the meaning of these policy positions is more than the sum of their parts, as the opponents of the change may be even more aware than its proponents. The relationships between the power of the state and capitalist relations, and between alternative ways of accounting for this relationship are at issue. Official power can support economic life in different ways and the different ways can be justified. There has been a long period in which government has been viewed as the problem not the solution, while in a new period the importance of official action has been highlighted. This is a basic difference, shaping long periods of public policy and of how citizens relate to society at large and to each other. And as official policy and legitimate state power move in one direction, alternative associational power linked to other accounts, for example of the Tea Party Movement, moves in the other direction.

Change is most apparent when it comes to questions of the relationship between the long history of racism and American democracy, what I have been calling here the American dilemma. Obama has attempted to identify the American story with the overcoming of the dilemma and more broadly identifying the story of America with the struggles for social justice. Official anti-racist policy is embodied by the President. His speech and actions are often interpreted in these terms, for better or worse. Things have been turned around, revealed not only in positive official advancements, but also in the confusion of public discussions about the President and his actions, as in Gates-gate. The legitimate anti-racist position of the federal government now is supported by the highest ranking public authority. It is sometimes challenged by oppositional movements wanting to take America back, with very different imaginations of what America is and what it should be. The explanation of the appeal of Sarah Palin is that she effectively presents and embodies this imagination, as we have seen here. The culture, the story about America is being changed, and the new story is being resisted.

Most strikingly, we have seen changes in the way politics have been done in the recent past in America. Participation is now a key support for political action. Obama prevailed in the Primaries and in the general election because his candidacy was adopted by a developing social movement, building on the anti-war movement of the Bush years and the way of doing Democratic Party politics developed around the candidacy of Howard Dean. Now the opposition to Obama is taking the same form in the Tea Party movement. This is a structural change, a way of utilizing the type of power in which Arendt was most interested, connected to different, indeed opposing, cultural positions.

And the most striking characteristic of Obama as a public persona: he has demonstrated that classical rhetoric skills and eloquence can make a difference in the present media and political world. He shows that there is an alternative to sound-bite politics, as his opponents have used innovative media strategies to attack him. What is remarkable is the degree to which careful reasoned appeals have been effective, although they are not always or even usually so. I am not claiming that deliberate careful persuasion has now triumphed. Rather the transformation is that it has been shown to have a chance. Fox presents an important base of resistance to this transformation, to be sure, but that classical eloquence is an important part of twenty-first-century American culture represents a significant case of reinvention, with the power of culture working in significant ways against a culture of power.

4

Spaces of Possibility in the Middle
East: Seeking Reinvention in Everyday
Practice

As we have seen, at key moments, political culture matters. The historic changes in the former Soviet bloc were shaped by alternative
relationships between power and culture forged by the democratic
opposition, i.e., "living in truth" as opposed to the official truth.
Barack Obama re-told the American story, and he and his supporters have worked to transform the local, national, and global politics
of the singular superpower. At these moments, political culture not
only mattered, it also was changed, although there were significant
resistances, as we observed in the last chapter. The Middle East is
a place where such resistance to change is most apparent, where
enduring patterns of political culture appear to be definitive, and
reinvention seems to be doomed to failure. Power and culture are
related in rigid ways, yielding tragedy and suffering.

Yet, such appearances can be deceiving. Reinvention is a
possibility even in such circumstances. In this chapter, we will
explore alternatives to tragedy and suffering, as political culture
is reinvented in everyday life. First, I will depict the depth of the
tragedy as it has developed on the central political stage. Then, I
will show how both the tragedy and the alternatives are embedded
in everyday practices, and the political culture that they generate.
This will permit us to examine strategic sites of reinvention, where
culture is not only a matter of destiny but also creativity, and
where the power of political culture includes not only that of the
truth regimes and their forms of legitimation, but also the power
of people acting in concert against official scripts.

The Tragedy

Storytelling and memory practices are a key to the conflict in the Middle East. The way each group tells its story and remembers its past is intimately tied with power, of the state and of resistance, in military and in collective action. The way each group depicts the other further rigidifies the power configuration. There is a long history here, although not as long as some purport, and it points to the enduring conflict.

The Israeli Story and Orientalism: The Jews have been persecuted for millennia. Exile has brought discrimination, persecution, pogroms, and the Shoah. To have a country of their own, in the historic biblical homeland, has realized religious aspirations along with secular dreams. For the religious, there has been ambivalence: to be in the land of Israel seemed to fulfill God's plan for the Jewish people, but to do so through secular means has been viewed by some as an abomination, at first by the majority, later by a significant minority. For the secular, also, there was far from unanimity concerning modern Zionism. Zionism before the Holocaust was a minority position. Most Jews immigrated to Israel fleeing pogroms, the Holocaust, and anti-Semitism of one sort or another, from North Africa to Russia. They did so more because they were pushed out, rather than pulled in. But there was a pull. To have a country of their own, to be strong, instead of weak, in the making of this country was the modern nationalist answer to the deprivations of the Diaspora. After the Holocaust, this became the opinion of the overwhelming majority. Jews in a state of their own could be strong, the major key of the Zionist Revisionists, and could realize dreams of social justice in a Jewish homeland, the key of the Labor Zionists. They could go to a land which was purported to be with no people (or at least a land where the people were not of large number and were not fully utilizing the land's promise) for a people with no land.

Confronting the other, the Arab Palestinian inhabitants, presented a key problem. Theodor Herzl imagined in his classic text, *Der Judenstaat* ("The State of the Jews"), that the coming of advanced European people to Palestine would bring civilization and social development to the region, and thus mutual benefit and peace to the newcomers and the indigenous people. This Eurocentric colonialist view proved to be far from the case when Herzl's dreams of a Jewish state became a reality, first, in the form of immigration and Jewish settlement, and then nation state building, and alternative views set in. From the romantic notions that the Palestinians were descendants of the ancient Hebrews (popular in the 1920s) to antagonistic views that sought to expel the Palestinian Arab population from the Land of Israel, from benign to malignant, "Orientalism" was a common thread.

The Palestinian Story and Occidentalism: Palestinians are the Israeli story's victims. The founding of the state of Israel is understood and commemorated as Al-Nakba, the Day of Catastrophe. The Jewish national project challenged the Palestinian Arab presence. Land that was bought, taken, and settled led to Palestinian Arab displacement. The British colonial commitment to a Jewish homeland in the Balfour Declaration compromised Palestinian Arab claims to their own land. The UN resolution recognizing the partition of historic Palestine into a Jewish state and a Palestinian state meant that a people who occupied only 8 percent of the land were given 55 percent, while the majority was denied its sovereign rights over their own homes, villages, and fields. With each advance in the development of the Jewish state, there were losses for the Palestinian people – expulsion and occupation, loss of property and rights, and loss of life itself. Each war led to further devastation, and even the peace process and the pursuit of reconciliation, required Palestinian deprivations. Every time there have been negotiations, more sacrifice has been required of the Palestinians. They have been the victims of European colonialism and its legacies, and they have not been able to escape its grip. They, and not the perpetrators of oppression and atrocity, have had to pay for European anti-Semitism and genocide.

The Palestinian history of resistance is a heroic struggle, not without mistakes (for a sober account see Khalidi, 2007). Their pursuit of justice, whether understood from a nationalist, Islamic, or human rights perspective, persists. They see the Israeli Jews as the enemy: some have dreamt of a unified Palestinian homeland with the expulsion of the Israelis; others dream of a secular bi-national state where citizens of all religions live with equal rights and responsibilities; yet others of a two-state solution, in which Palestinians will have a state of their own. Yet, dealing with the Jews as European colonizers, as part of a Western project to divide the Arab world and seize strategic ground, an Occidentalist view, is something that Palestinians of all political positions agree upon.

The Palestinian and the Israeli narratives each are linked to the enactment of local and global power. The Palestinian notion of justified and mandated resistance demanded the Intifadas of 1987–92 and 2000–4, as well as the earlier moments of resistance dating back to 1917. When a peaceful status quo is understood as being a continuation of occupation and suffering, resistance, violent and non-violent, is required. It is a way of not only protesting, fighting against an unacceptable situation, by any means necessary, but of defending oneself and one's honor. It is not simply a question of political tactics, achieving a specific political goal, independence, the realization of Palestinian rights. It is a matter of identity. If one resists, one exists. If one does not, there is cultural death. There is no alternative to resistance. The story told leads directly to political and military action, to resistance of all sorts.

And for the Israeli, such resistance is an ongoing threat. There is no alternative to self-defense and the pursuit of security. The establishment of a Jewish state is a great accomplishment, but it is insecure. While the international community endorsed the partition of historic Palestine, it has been unsteady in its support of the defense of Israel. The Jewish people cannot depend upon the good will of others. Israel is surrounded by hostile neighbors, and the threat of attack from their neighbors and Palestinians, from outside, but also from within Israeli borders, is an ongoing reality. There is little room for error. Vigilance is a matter of national survival and personal safety. The Palestinians and their Arab supporters deny the legitimacy of the Jewish state, and the international community beyond the region does not adequately understand, does not respect, what this means. Self-defense in the form of a powerful military defense force is paramount, with, in recent years, the invasion of Lebanon, the war in Gaza, and other such aggressive actions a necessity, despite the human suffering involved.

Each side holds a coherent position, with a plurality of alternative voices. No loyal Palestinian, no matter how committed to coexistence, can question the value of resistance. No loyal Israeli, no matter how understanding of the plight of the Palestinians, can question the importance of security. There is a logic to each position, and their relationships, that is next to impossible to escape. When these core values are questioned, the questioner loses political standing. Each alternative position in the political sphere has to be articulated using these core values. This solidifies the impasse. It appears center stage and at the margins. Resistance compromises security. Security disallows resistance. The conflict is radicalized and common ground appears impossible as a result.

Yet, there are Israeli and Palestinian peace camps, and the significance of this has been recognized by Israelis and Palestinians. Edward Said in "Truth and Reconciliation," a 1999 article published in *Al-Ahram Weekly,* noted that religious and right-wing Israelis, those bent on domination of the Palestinians as the way to security and justice, are not the only Israelis. "For others, who want peace as a result of reconciliation . . . Many such Israelis demonstrate energetically against their government's Palestinian land expropriations and house demolitions. So one senses a healthy willingness to look elsewhere for peace than in land-grabbing and suicide-bombs." He goes on to observe and then recommend: "Yet, feelings of persecution, suffering and victimhood are so ingrained [among Palestinians and Israelis] that it is nearly impossible to undertake political initiatives that hold Jews and Arabs to the same general principles of civil equality while avoiding the pitfalls of us-versus-them. Palestinian intellectuals need to express their case directly to Israelis in public forums, universities, and the media. The challenge is both to and within civil society which long has been subordinate to a nationalism that has developed into an obstacle to reconciliation" (Said, 1999).

But Said's democratic, civil, anti-nationalist, anti-military position, taken before the second Intifada, reveals the dimension of the problem after the Intifada. In the name of resistance, there is now a Palestinian boycott of Israeli cultural as well as political institutions. And because of such resistance, Israelis "against their government's Palestinian land expropriations and house demolitions," find themselves isolated from their compatriots, because they think that such expressions of dissent undermine the resolute commitment to national security and survival.

The civil project, Said's project, thus, on both sides, seems to be impossible. In order for it to work, Palestinians have to engage the Israeli public, but at this point any such moves are discouraged in the name of resistance. Those who engage the Israeli public, who engage in dialogue with Israeli partners, are vulnerable to being labeled collaborators. And Israelis who argue against occupation and domination, those who question the treatment of Palestinians at checkpoints, who demonstrate against the Separation Wall, who are critical of Israeli military actions in Lebanon and Gaza, are viewed by their compatriots as, at best, dreamers, who do not understand the central importance of security. Israeli politicians who attempt to seriously engage with Palestinian partners, who question military calculations as the primary avenue to security, are destined to lose support.[46] Citizen initiatives that are committed to these positions are viewed by some as naïve and by others as treasonous. This is the political culture of the tragedy.

Two rights, two competing notions of memory and justice, confront each other in mortal and apparently eternal conflict. Nonetheless, a closer look at the conflict in its specific manifestations reveals a more complex situation, including alternatives. Checkpoints are locations where the conflict is most clearly manifest, where the tragedy is most apparent. It would seem to be the least likely of places to discover alternatives, but, as I will demonstrate, because they can be discerned when we look closely, it is especially significant.

A Checkpoint[47]

Checkpoints are to be found throughout the Palestinian occupied territories. The occupying authorities use them to maintain control over the movements of the local population. They control movement between Israel and the territories. They control areas surrounding settlements. They, along with the restricted road system, provide easy movement through the territories for Israelis. And they impede movement from one Palestinian area to another. In sum, they are primary instruments of the occupation. Here the two narratives confront each other, revealing the tragedy in everyday life. But also here unexpected things are going on. For the Palestinians, while this is a place primarily of subjugation, it is also a place where resistance in its variety is revealed and in fact is debated. For the Israelis, while this is a place that maintains security and safety for the Jewish nation state, it is also a place where the ways of confronting the other, in a variety of different forms, are apparent. The tragic confrontation of the dominant narratives is present, but also there are the alternative possibilities.

The checkpoint is first a place of control and confrontation. Consider Rema Hammami's description of the Surda checkpoint:

> For almost three years, the final leg of the commute between Birzeit University and Ramallah meant a one- to two-kilometre walk through the obstacle course of rubble mounds and concrete blocks of the no-drive zone known as the Surda checkpoint. On either side, knots of transit vans jammed into the narrow road waiting to carry passengers off to their final destination (for many travelers, this was simply another checkpoint). The worst days were those when trigger-happy Israeli soldiers suddenly prohibited the stream of travelers from this daily hike, and literally thousands of students on one side and as many villagers on the other were stuck. More usually, soldiers set up shop a few hours a day and toyed with the droves of walking commuters – stopping all or a select few for interminable searches of bags or identity cards, or trying to "organize" the transit vans and checkpoint peddlers by ramming into their stands or vehicles with their jeeps. At the checkpoint three people were shot to death by the Israeli military, another two died in traffic accidents among the crush of transit vans, at least one man died of a heart attack as he was wheeled across on a metal stretcher, two babies were born behind a rubble mound, untold numbers of young men were beaten by soldiers – often in full view of everyone – and no one can count the numbers of injured at the demonstrations that were staged in a futile attempt to get rid of the thing.

The dynamics of social interaction implied by this passage are significant. They establish a particular truth regime, as Michel Foucault would highlight, and a shared set of attitudes legitimating the prevailing pattern of domination, as would be the concern of Max Weber, with an apparently stable definition of the situation, as would be the concern of Erving Goffman, as a student of W. I. Thomas.[48] But when we look more closely, tactical and performative alternatives do appear, the possibilities of concerted public action are there to be observed. The discipline, the legitimation, and the performance each contribute to the political culture.

Discipline

Israeli arms and the logic of occupation establish a truth regime. They are two sides of the same coin. The need to control terrorism and armed insurrection justifies the disciplinary practices of the occupation. In this regime, power and culture are closely brought together. Armed resistance is identified as terror. Armed occupation is understood as defense. The enactment of knowledge and power establishes the realities of the conflict. Acts of non-violent resistance are perceived as armed resistance in the making, and also can be and are seen as terror or support of terror. The harassment of ordinary people trying to get on with their daily life, thus, becomes a military necessity. Any form of explicit resistance can be understood as insurrection. Such is Foucault at the checkpoint.

Foucault's position on power is not directly related to or translatable into the workings of the state from the center of its authority to the peripheries. Rather, power must be articulated at the ground level in human practices. At the checkpoint, the classical political understanding of the state and its monopolization of violence, as Weber understood this, are, to be sure, present. The overwhelming military superiority, its official use, by the occupation forces is the context of action. But how this superiority is present is much more problematic than is ordinarily understood. There is a situationally specific dimension to this. Power is created in the situation as the amplification of the occupying power, as a constituting force of occupation. But specific agents, to a significant degree, independently from centralized authority, create this power in a specific place, and they constitute the direction and quality of power.

The checkpoint is filled with ambiguity. It is dense with a variety of different social agents. There are the soldiers, border police, and travelers. There are taxis and porters, those who move the travelers, and there are those who watch the comings and goings and checkings, including human rights activists. Often the checkpoint is isolated, an outpost. It is meant to create security and to enact control. Enemies of the state are to be weeded out, potential terrorists, suicide bombers chief among them. The full repressive control of the occupation authorities can be utilized. But as the soldiers check, they are outnumbered, and potentially quite vulnerable to military attack, and to violent protest. While an outpost for security, the checkpoint reeks of insecurity, both among the checked and among the checkers. The power in the hands of the checkers is not just a representation of central authority. It is produced in the locality. Nir Gazit explains:

> The state's central administration (i.e. politicians and high-ranking state officials) may act as a directive agency, and yet it intentionally limits its direct power by dispersing its authority to its various agents in the field. This is not a mere governmental decentralization, where the state bureaucracy expands and branches out; rather, it is a shift in a governmental locus of control. Hence, in absence of formal definitions regarding the political status of the occupied space and its associated sites, the political routine in the occupied territories is subjected to discontinuous political and violent practices and changeable presuppositions. As a result, fragmented sovereignty is a complex and elusive political institutionalization of power, constituted through ongoing social processes. Power and authority are not simply given attributes. They are fluctuating dynamics that are constantly manufactured, reproduced and changed by the practices of ground-level agents. (Gazit, n.d.)

Given the uncertainties of the checkpoint, and that the local agents are equipped to manage them, using both officially approved and unapproved means, these agents have the power to govern and control, to "discipline," to enact "governmentality," in Foucault's terms. This is a significant dimension of the political culture of the checkpoint.

The disciplinary power and resistance to it at the checkpoint are intimately connected with cultural accounts and motivations. For the soldiers assigned to this duty, it cannot be very pleasant. Day in day out, they interfere with the comings and goings of ordinary people in their everyday pursuits. The guards are there to protect the security of their nation, but mostly they create insecurity for the people with whom they interact. Strong convictions concerning the Israeli narrative sustain the guards' actions and help them to overcome the tedium and unpleasantness of their tasks.

For the Palestinian passers-by, the guards are the personification of all that they are against. They are not only everyday obstacles in their daily life, sources of great inconvenience and discomfort. They embody the power of occupation and oppression. In order for Palestinians to get to the office, the doctor, the market, back home, or visit a friend, the Israeli officials must be treated gingerly, but they should not be given too much respect because resisting them is a primary political imperative and matter of identity and dignity. Here there is a deadly side to the ordinary games of deference and demeanor, which are a normal part of everyday life (Goffman, 1967: 47–96). This points to the importance of considering another way that the political culture of the checkpoint is constituted, having more to do with social control, than with discipline.

Social Control and Legitimation

There is a kind of control that is not part of, goes beyond, discipline. It is a kind of power that is more interactively related to culture. People are socialized into the order of things. Power prevails, but people must act in the situations they enter in an informed fashion. Entering the situation, they learn what the roles of the different social actors are and what the attitudes of these actors are toward each other. To get on with their lives, they then act accordingly, legitimating but also challenging prevailing power relations. This action has both expected and unexpected results.

When new members of the checkpoint scene enter, be they functionaries of the occupation or the occupied, they must learn how to behave.[49] Beyond the imperatives of security and resistance, the rules of the game must be understood and followed in order to get on with everyday tasks. The checkpoint officers must learn who is to be considered for "special treatment" and who is to be treated more routinely, how to identify a potential threat and how to act when faced with such a threat, how and when to assert authority, and how and when to retreat and be conciliatory to the monitored and the controlled. Action in situationally appropriate ways keeps the checkpoint functioning, as it both permits and disrupts movement. Misunderstanding the attitudes of others can cause problems, even fatal ones. People learn the attitudes of the other towards themselves, how others will act towards them, and then act accordingly. In this way, apart from discipline, there is legitimation, social control, and its disruption. This is an important field of political culture.

A great deal that transpires day to day involves social control, the control of action by the participants themselves. The looming powers of occupation and resistance are there, to be sure, but there are also the quotidian regularities. New border guards learn how to do their job, becoming familiar with how to respond to the challenges of human rights observers, developing cool authority in the face of hot humanitarian challenges, from the doctors and teachers who need to get to their work, to the patients and students who seek their services. Those who are impeded learn how they can maximize their chances to get through, what arguments and evidence to present, how to carry themselves and their baggage (metaphoric and actual). The humanitarian workers, when they are present, mediate. As they observe the comings and goings, they are struck by a critical question: do they control the abuses of the checkpoint regime or are they agents in the machine who facilitate its smooth functioning? As they interact in a normal regularized fashion with the authorities, they monitor what the authorities will do openly. The unseasoned guard resents this, but the seasoned guard uses the relatively good relations the monitors have with the Palestinians to assert control. This, the Palestinians and the monitors understand, leads to ambivalence in their relationships. The people of the checkpoint understand each other to a considerable degree, and act accordingly, but there is also a high degree of uncertainty, which also controls. This is the power of terror.

Terror's power is not the power to assert harsh punishments upon the guilty, but also upon the innocent, as Hannah Arendt brilliantly demonstrated in "Ideology and Terror," the final chapter of her *The Origins of Totalitarianism* (1968). The checkpoint authorities use the always possible closure of the checkpoint and the always possible refusal of passage and even arrest to any one passer-by, to exact compliance. The power to create uncertainty and to resolve it, independently of the other, establishes harsh control, a distinctive political culture. Thus the dynamics of social control and of discipline are closely related. Yet, they are not absolute.

Performance and Definition

The distinction between regime strategy and daily tactics, highlighted by de Certeau, reveals an opening in the system of discipline and social control. He is particularly interested in how disciplinary regimes, such as the occupation, are limited. The Israelis set up the checkpoints as instruments of the occupation. The Israeli state has the power to conduct its operation. It decides where and when the checkpoints are located. The rules permitting some people to pass through, while others are stopped, who will be interrogated and who will be arrested, are a matter of military-state policy and situational circumstances. But the way the rules will function will also depend on the people involved on both sides of the operation, and upon those who are in a position to observe the operation. The way they act matters. The knowledge, the culture that informs their actions, is a significant dimension of the political culture.

Travelers know when they can drive and when they must walk. They know what kinds of documents and permits are required to move things by automobile, and they know when they can do so. They know where they can drive, where horse and carts are permitted, and where they can only walk and carry things by hand. The checkpoint rupture in easy movement from one place to another has opened up opportunities of individual enterprise from taxis and minibuses to horse carts and pushcarts. And when the enterprise leads from competition to physical conflict, local toughs and Palestinian authorities have to enforce public order.

While there is much that is quite remarkable about all this, there is also much that is quite ordinary. The Israelis control Palestinian movement and activity, and the Palestinians develop tactics to get on with their lives. The conflicts at the checkpoint between Israelis and Palestinians involve face-to-face enactments of occupational politics. But the acts of cooperation are not as easy to understand, and there is conflict among Palestinians. One person's socialization into the system and collaboration is another's simple pursuit of survival, and given the political situation, survival with dignity can and is understood as resistance. To understand this complex structure, to understand the checkpoint as a public domain, as Rema Hammami (2005) suggests we should, requires looking at interaction not only as a system of discipline, social control, and tactical responses, but also as performance. Performance reveals the dynamic, uncertain qualities of political culture and there is no place where this is more evident than in zones of static confrontation, such as the checkpoint.

The establishment of the checkpoint regime severed the normal movement of people, goods, and services that made Palestinian social life, its education, economics, and politics, possible. Alongside the Israeli project of occupation, informed by ideas of security, Palestinians have struggled to establish and maintain a system of transportation that helped ordinary citizens to move about. A system of taxis, minibuses, and porters became together an informal public transportation system for people, goods, and services. This system formed and has functioned through everyday interactions, combining coercion and cooperation between Israelis and Palestinians, and separately among Israelis and among Palestinians. People have adapted to this very odd situation by establishing relatively clear rules of the game. Though the meaning of what they do is a matter of conflict, they do it in regular ways.

Initially, Hammami reports, individual improvised acts attempted to link severed movement channels, but then, given the absence of grassroots organizations, networks of informal workers developed among themselves an alternative system of movement. She observes:

> Thus, the unlikely symbols of the new steadfastness are not the "national institutions" such as the schools, but rather the sub-proletariat of Ford transit van drivers. Considered a menace on the roads and lawbreakers during normal times, now their anarchic, semi-criminal bravado subculture (exemplified by the ubiquitous Nike "No Fear" stickers they place on their back windshields) are a testament to the ethic of getting through anything, by anything, and to anywhere despite all obstacles. It is the same masculine lumpenproletariat subculture of the van drivers that has been in many ways the backbone of the informal organizing systems developed to make it possible for individuals to "get there." (Hammami, 2005)

A regime of control enforced its rules. But as the regime operated, those who were disciplined by it, who had to move about, developed tactics to get on with their lives, despite the regime.

But the political meaning of these activities is far from clear. While Hammami identifies the realization of a collective persistence and dignity, others see collaboration. And the drivers themselves and the soldiers at the checkpoints work to define their project in one direction and in the other. How the transit workers present themselves to each other and to the occupational authorities involves ongoing processes of the presentations of self in everyday life and definitions of situations, as Goffman would highlight. The political stakes in this are high. A culture of everyday resistance is open to the most ordinary of people in their everyday lives.

Hammami tells the story of Zaid and Abu Abed, organizers of the transit workers at the Surda checkpoint. The Abed brothers established and held their positions as local toughs, with the support of the authorities. They had to maintain order in an inherently chaotic situation by managing three main problems: controlling who got to work, controlling their competition, and managing the Israeli soldiers and their potential acts of destruction. These obviously fulfilled the interests of the Palestinian general population to get from here to there, the interests of the workers to get work fairly and decently, and the interest of the occupation forces, to have the system of control work. Looking closely at the way they did this, along with their colleagues and the authorities, we observe a struggle for political definition. The struggle over the definition of the situation is a key element of the political culture of the checkpoint.

The soldiers would attempt to use Zaid to control the taxi operation. He reported:

> In the beginning, the soldiers would come and ask that I tell the drivers to back off from the rubble mound five meters, or tell me they should be as far back as the electrical pole. I'd tell the drivers, "The soldiers are demanding one, two, three and you have to move back as far as the pole." Whoever pulled back, pulled back and whoever didn't had their keys and IDs taken. But then I got sick of it, agitated. A soldier called me over and said, "Tell the drivers to move up." I said to him, "Listen, do I work for you as an employee? Every day, you call me over. Come here. Go there. [. . .] I'm just the organizer of the Birzeit cars." He took my identity card and made me sit. It was winter, and I sat for three hours in the rain. He said, "That's so you're taught a lesson and learn." I told him, "Nevertheless, you call me over again and I'm not going to answer. It's not my job." (Hammami, 2005)

The soldiers attempted to use the organizers to extend their powers by fostering indirect control. This obviously served a practical task, but it also symbolically expressed a definition of who was in control and who was subservient. Zaid resisted, presenting himself as an independent Palestinian, not kowtowing to the Israeli military. In some ways, he did not really change the situation, but he did change its definition and his apparent role in it. For appearance sake, which is not to say without good reason,

Zaid and his brother understood this and attempted to maintain their independence and dignity. They preferred a Druze soldier who used brute force to exact compliance.

Involved here is a little game of legitimacy, with potentially big symbolic significance. Although the general population in the occupied territories certainly does not believe in the legitimacy of the occupation, if Palestinians organize themselves and act according to the rules of the occupation game, without, at least, symbolic acts of defiance, the regime establishes an appearance of legitimacy in daily practices (since what appears in politics is reality, as Arendt demonstrates);[50] they would in their actions confirm the Israeli narrative. If on the other hand, the regime functions in such a way that it permits Palestinians to get on with their lives with the public appearance of gestures of defiance, the legitimacy is subverted in daily practices. The Palestinian narrative would appear to the Palestinians and to the Israeli officials. A political culture of resistance is confirmed. At the checkpoint, when everything goes smoothly, when Zaid helps organize the drivers so they can move their clients across the restricted terrain, the normality of the occupation is confirmed. When he visibly questions that normality, and the Israeli soldiers have to manage movements knowing that he will, the normality is regularly questioned. And if the operation occurs with the public appearance of force, again the normality is revealed to be a lie. And as this appears in public, its significance is debated by those involved and also by observers.

Thus in the case of Surda, clients and passers-by of the transporters (both drivers of vehicles and porters helping people carry the disabled, children, and heavy objects through the checkpoint zone) were watching, drawing the conclusion that the system amounted to collaboration. One porter who made money on helping people get by a closed checkpoint, Mustapha, remembered his experiences:

> I got sick of it. The work was going well, but ... I was ready to drop it, because there wasn't a single person passing who didn't say, "Exploiter" or "You're the ones that are keeping the checkpoint [i.e., the road] closed." The girls from the university would pass by and

say, "You're the cause of the checkpoint." I got sick, ill, [from] people calling us collaborators. One day I was carrying a man, young, a clerk, in the carriage and he starts saying to me, "You guys don't want the checkpoint to open, do you? You're the ones that want to close it. You're the cause of the closure." And he's riding back there! I pulled the bridle of the horse and grabbed him by the shirt and told him to get out. He'd given me five shekels and I said to him "Here's your five shekels, I'm throwing it in the valley, and here's five shekels from my pocket, and don't you dare try and ride with me again. I'll slaughter you." (Hammami, 2005)

And this had a class dimension. Periodically there were open acts of resistance against the checkpoint. Students would throw rocks, and the Israeli soldiers would respond. Bullets and guns would damage the windows of vans and cars of the drivers. Hammami notes:

The clear class difference between demonstrating students from the university and the sub-proletariat of van drivers and porters only served to accentuate the latter's contention that middle-class kids (who "didn't know how to fight properly" anyway) were simply creating a mess for those needing to pass or the poor trying to make a living. (2005)

The way people go about creating a transportation system between the demands of the occupying authorities and the demands for resistance marks the distinction between the appearance of a political culture of resistance, of steadfastness, and subordination. And appearing to "fight properly," appearing to respect the need to get on with life and to earn a living, the exact ways these things are performed, make for the appearance of resistance and not self-destruction.

Hammami concludes:

[The] more significant resistance could be found in the less dramatic but tenacious everyday subversion of the checkpoint regime itself. Checkpoint workers constantly subverted physical boundaries: at night they stealthily pushed concrete blocks a few more inches apart to make way for horse carriages, or trampled the edges of newly-made dirt barriers so that porter carts could get to the other side. And through both necessity and ingenuity, they reclaimed the space of the checkpoint from being purely a site of oppression and brutality into one where livelihood, social life and even sociability could be recovered. (2005)

This is a theoretically striking conclusion, pointing to the potential significance of the politics of everyday life. The checkpoint is a central instrument of the occupation. The micropolitics of discipline and social control, though, do not tell the whole story. Through situational tactics and the politics of performance, it is a place of struggle, even a kind of public domain. It is one of the primary sites where domination is enacted on a daily basis, where the Israeli narrative is confirmed. Yet, even in such a place, there are alternative possibilities, alternative narratives are written in everyday practices.

Alternatives Beyond the Checkpoints: the Palestinians

Let's shift a bit and consider how Palestinians have consciously used the performances of daily life in reinventing their political culture, not just as a matter of defense, but much more positively. The Orient House is a good place to start.

The Orient House has been one of the most prominent civil society organizations in which these complicated games of presentation and interpretation have played a central role in Palestinian history, particularly the history of Jerusalem. A historic structure, built as a private residence in 1897 for Ismail Musa Al-Husseini, it became a central location for micropolitics in 1983. According to the Orient House's website, in that year, Faisal Husseini rented space in the building to set up offices for the Arab Studies Society "for archives, press data, statistics, etc."[51] But this presentation, this politically benign definition of the situation of the organization, has been generally understood as a kind of gaming with the Israeli authorities. Nazmi Al-Ju'beh observes:

While society continued to work on documentation and research on Jerusalem and the Arab-Israeli conflict, it also succeeded in developing itself into a major political voice for Palestinians in East Jerusalem and, on certain issues, for all Palestinians in the Occupied Territories. The founder, in part capitalizing on the reputation of his illustrious family history,[52] managed to gain high credibility among the people. The late eighties witnessed the rise of Faisal al-Hussaini from local Palestinian leader to an international figure through his early preparation for the negotiations of the peace process.

The newly established political center came to be known as the Orient House, a designation that symbolized the status of the center and reflected the crowning achievement of a long political process in Jerusalem: it was ample demonstration of the weakness of the Israeli control of East Jerusalem. It is very difficult to imagine the breakthrough 1990–1 in the peace process without taking into account the role of the Orient House on every level – Palestinians in the Occupied Territories, in the diaspora (especially the Palestinian leadership in Tunisia), as well as on both the Israeli and United States fronts.

The rise of the Orient House is to be seen as the result of a long institutional building process of the civil society; as well, it filled the vacuum created by the Israeli policy to dissolve the Arab municipality and other Palestinian institutions in Jerusalem. So the Orient House became a political and institutional umbrella for the Palestinians in Jerusalem as well as in the rest of the Occupied Territories. (Al-Ju'beh, 2003)

Controversy surrounded Orient House. It served multiple functions, and was presented as such. For the Palestinians of Jerusalem, it was defined by the social agents in the house as a center of political life, and it became such. The house was presented as a purely cultural institution, and it was presented as the effective seat of Palestinian authority in its future capital. Meetings among Palestinians, between Palestinians and Israelis, and with foreign delegations occurred in the house. To open the house as an independent center, it was presented as a purely civil cultural institution, which it was. With the absence of the Arab municipality and other Palestinian institutions in Jerusalem, it became a kind of capital building. For both of these things to happen, for the cultural center to exist and political functions to be sustained, people interacted with each other performing these terms. As is true of social life in general, people defined something as real, and it was real in its consequences, as W.I. Thomas put it.[53] When foreign dignitaries arrived, people interacted as if this were an official gathering between them and the authorities of a legitimate, recognized Palestinian state. Such performative accomplishments created facts on the ground within annexed Jerusalem. Ultimately this was unacceptable to the Israeli government of Ariel Sharon.

Such a field of presentation and definition is the micro-infrastructure of social life and a key site for reinventing political culture. Presentations, offerings, are made to the powers, and this has consequences, but there is also room for creative alternative presentations of self and definitions of the situation that can be of even greater importance. People meet with each other and make presentations in their everyday life. The purpose of the presentation may not be just to sustain a working definition of the situation, the case that Goffman focused on, but also to move the definition, to open it up as a way of acting politically. Such action was centrally focused on the Orient House at a certain moment, it was a specific site for the reinvention of political culture, but it has become a more general project.

Hammami makes the connection between small interactions and the major political confrontations as they are now presented. There are the strategies and tactics of the occupiers and occupied. Performance in daily life enacts both, as it addresses the pressing conflict. Hammami notes that a primary strategic goal of nationalist Palestinian ideology has been *sumud,* steadfastness. In the seventies that goal meant "staying on the land and refusing to leave despite the hardships of occupation." It became during the Second Intifada *al hayaat lazim yistami*, "life must go on." This, she explains, is a response to a collective understanding that the general strikes of the First Intifada actually weakened Palestinian society, destroying businesses and undermining the education of a generation of children. "This time, schools, universities, and workplaces have all made staying open their rallying cry. In so doing, they helped set the framework for much of the society to follow in the collectively understood, but individually achieved daily resistance of simply getting there." In the aftermath of the Second Intifada, the project of life going on has been applied throughout daily life, including in the most unlikely of places, the interactive world of the checkpoint, and other spaces where the occupation is expressed and resisted in daily practices.

Micropolitics, thus, have made and continue to make up a rich political field, and, in my judgment, this is the location of the most significant political action among Israelis and Palestinians, where the tragic confrontation of security versus resistance can be avoided. As the visible conventional politics of the peace process and of armed struggle and defense, and state building are stalemated, the forces of occupation and armed resistance confront each other, and alternatives to both are revealed in micropolitics off the center stage. The alternatives are to be found, as reinventing political culture becomes a possibility in a broad micro-political domain. At the checkpoint and beyond, there is discipline and control and resistance, but also something else can be observed: a ground for direct political challenge and the purposeful constitution of alternatives, a setting for the reinvention of political culture.

Reinvention Beyond the Checkpoints: The Israelis and Palestinians

People in the micro-political terrain can and do come together and develop a capacity to act in concert, constituting power, sometimes the power of the powerless, and the potential is there for the most mundane interactions to lead to historic changes. The politics of small things, emerging from the micro-political terrain, can matter, significantly because the relationship between knowledge and power is changed, and the kind of cultural understandings of politics and the cultural grounding for political action are transformed.

And this involves not only the empowerment of one side of the conflict, as described thus far, but, in fact, also how the two sides meet. Consider an occasion when a reinvented political culture stood as a clear alternative to the politics of coercion and force, the happenings on April 24, 2006, in city of Dahab, Sinai, a site of the terrorist attacks. A *New York Times* report described the facts: "Three blasts tore through Dahab, a crowded resort town on the Sinai Peninsula, on Monday night, killing at least 30 people and wounding more than 115." This was one of three such attacks, on Taba and Sharm el Sheik, as well. In Dahab there were three targets: the Nelson Restaurant, the Aladdin Café, and the Ghazala Supermarket were all hit within five minutes. While the bombings were not large, they caused great damage. "Bodies were every-where," said Ahmed el Tabakh, who said he ran into the middle of the chaos moments after the blast near the supermarket. "We carried bodies until the government came" (Slackman, 2006). Worldwide attention was focused on the terrorists who attacked and on the military response by the Egyptian authorities. What incited the terrorists to attack this particular place was not given much attention.

Dahab is a place of casual fraternization. In its restaurants, nightclubs, and bars, Egyptians and Israelis, along with global trekkers of a great variety of nationalities, talk, joke, and dance with each other. As they have socialized, they have been establish-ing important facts on the ground, quite different ones than those of settlers and terrorists, and the checkers and the checked of the checkpoint. In the Middle East, especially in Israel and in the Palestinian territories, such fraternization is an achievement with significant political importance. And it supports significant and principled interactions among people to act in concert with each other for political ends. People of the region, Muslims, Christians, and Jews, Palestinians and Israelis, can and do interact with each other in ways that point beyond violent conflict and international deadlock. Sometimes this leads to concerted actions monitoring and protesting the checkpoints, the Separation Wall and terrorist actions. Sometimes it involves secession from such confrontations. People meet each other, often against the common sense of their compatriots, define their meeting in new and distinctive ways and can create apart from the powers important facts on the ground.

It is the setting of interaction as a rich field of political possibility that provides the grounds for their power.[54]

The most visible and clearly political instance of this principled unofficial interaction has been the Geneva Agreements. Independent Palestinian and Israeli diplomats came together, apart from formal government structures, and spelled out what is obvious to almost all observers looking for a just settlement, the outlines of the two-state solution of the Arab-Israeli conflict. The exercise was criticized for undermining official negotiations, for being misguided, naïve, and too idealistic. But the apparent *naïveté*, its idealism, is actually a form of realism when we consider the target of the bombs in the Sinai. The initiative's conclusions spell out the logic of the life experience of the party-goers of Dahab. They are establishing the social patterns that perform and represent a peaceful settlement in their mundane interactions. This is clearly evident when we look at many social activities that have cooperation in solving social and cultural problems as their first principle and their goal.

There are dozens of Arab-Israeli and specifically Palestinian-Israeli groups working beyond the confines of political divisions on a regular everyday basis. These do not make headlines, but their meaning is of profound significance. They probably include more people than those who are directly involved with suicide bombings and reprisals. And recent history suggests that in such actions "the politics of small things," can have historic consequence. In the political movement for peace, in education, in cultural life, Palestinians and Israelis constitute political alternatives in their daily life.

As observed in the introduction, "The Parent Circle-Families Forum," an organization of bereaved Palestinian and Israeli families, with two centers, one serving primarily Israeli families in Tel Aviv, the other serving Palestinians, in East Jerusalem, supports reconciliation and tolerance. They are seeking to ensure that their losses to war, occupation, and terrorism do not serve as the basis of a politics of retribution. "Neve Shalom/Wahat al-Salam" (Oasis of Peace) is a cooperative village of Jews and Palestinian Arabs of Israeli citizenship situated equidistant from Jerusalem and Tel Aviv-Jaffa. With their bodies, they reveal the possibilities of coexistence. "Hope Flowers School," an independent school, in Bethlehem, West Bank, Palestine, works with young people in a special afternoon training curriculum on peace and democracy training. It proudly advertises that none of its graduates have been involved in suicide bombings, while they do engage in the struggle for social justice. "Sindyanna of Galilee," an economic organization led by women, combines commercial activity with community work. It stresses land preservation, environmental quality, women's empowerment, and women's labor rights. Staffed by Arab and Jewish women, who believe in a future of peace and prosperity for all people, it has worked to market goods produced in the occupied territories. "The Givat Haviva Institute" promotes equality and coexistence among the Jews and Arabs of Israel through wide educational programs for children and adults. On both sides of the Green Line, the Arab-Hebrew Theatre of Jaffa and the Freedom Theater of Jenin, use dramatic forms as an alternative to violence, as a constituted place for reflection and critical expression.

These are but a few of the everyday projects, along with the more explicitly political ones, concerned with the problems of human rights, the environment and reconciliation, that reveal what the former Czech dissident and president, Vaclav Havel (1985) called in a very different geo-political context, "the power of the powerless." As we have noted in chapter 2, back then and there, in Central Europe of the 1980s, people acted as if they lived in a free society and they created their own freedom, contributing to the fall of the Soviet empire, and helping constitute the democratic possibilities of post-Communism.[55] Now in Palestine and Israel, and in the Sinai, people are acting as if cooperation, mutual recognition, and respect are the norms, and for them they have become so. They present themselves to each other in this way, and they constitute alternative political realities. This is the potential social infrastructure of a just settlement of conflict, and it provides for both sides a democratic culture that can form a democratic post-settlement solution. We must pay close attention not only to the Dahab bombers and those who try to control them. We must pay attention to those who went to Dahab for a good time, and to those who try to build political projects around such normality.

Beyond Orientalism and Occidentalism: The Reinvention of Political Culture in Israel–Palestine

The tragedy of the Palestinian–Israeli conflict is in one sense very specific to the experience of Israelis and Palestinians, but on the other hand, it is part of a global story, often misleadingly labeled "the clash of civilizations." The larger story involves the traditions, practices, and antagonisms of Orientalism and Occidentalism, and the geo-politics of global terrorism and anti-terrorism. It is often asserted that the Israel–Palestine conflict is ground zero of these larger conflicts. Solve the Israeli-Palestinian conflict, and the conflicts between the Muslim world and the West would diminish. Let this conflict fester, and the clash of civilizations will escalate. Address the conflict and the fear of the East would diminish in the West, as would the fear of the West in the East. These propositions presuppose a notion of political culture that is too strong on inheritance, too weak on creativity, and is too totalized; a great deal of human suffering is the result. There is a sense that the reinvention of political culture, particularly in Israel–Palestine, is a pressing political problem, not only the reinvention of the specific political cultures but also a reinvention of our understanding of political culture. This is revealed in the idea of "the clash of civilizations."

Bernard Lewis coined the term in an essay provocatively entitled, "The Roots of Muslim Rage." His contention was that Islamic civilization has been in a state of crisis, brought on by resentment of the West:

> The Muslim has suffered successive stages of defeat. The first was his loss of domination in the world, to the advancing power of Russia and the West. The second was the undermining of his authority in his own country, through an invasion of foreign ideas and laws and ways of life and sometimes even foreign rulers or settlers, and the enfranchisement

of native non-Muslim elements. The third – the last straw – was the challenge to his mastery in his own house, from emancipated women and rebellious children. It was too much to endure, and the outbreak of rage against these alien, infidel, and incomprehensible forces that had subverted his dominance, disrupted his society, and finally violated the sanctuary of his home was inevitable. It was also natural that this rage should be directed primarily against the millennial enemy and should draw its strength from ancient beliefs and loyalties. Europe and her daughters? (Lewis, 1990)

This depiction of Muslim political culture is complete. The rage against Europe and its daughters, including centrally the United States as Lewis explains, is characterized as being irrational, a kind of civilizational pathology that we and they are going to have to live through. Our options are few. If we intervene, we may make matters worse, but we cannot ignore the problem.

Samuel Huntington, in his "The Clash of Civilizations?" draws the conclusion for global geo-politics:

It is my hypothesis that the fundamental source of conflict in this new world will not be primarily ideological or primarily economic. The great divisions among humankind and the dominating source of conflict will be cultural. Nation states will remain the most powerful actors in world affairs, but the principal conflicts of global politics will occur between nations and groups of different civilizations. The clash of civilizations will be the battle lines of the future. (Huntington, 1993)

Huntington took Lewis's thesis on Muslim rage and observed the same sort of clashes globally. There was a time when geo-politics was about conflict between rulers, monarchs, and emperors, following the Treaty of Westphalia. After the French Revolution, the conflict took the form of battle between nation states, and in the twentieth century, conflicts became primarily ideological between liberal democracy, fascism-Nazism, and Communism. It is Huntington's thesis that, in the twenty-first, conflicts have become civilizational, clearly from his point of view between the West and its enemies. It's a matter of political culture.

132

There is much that is problematic and controversial about this position. It divides the world into too neat camps. Huntington and Lewis both give deference to cultural diversity within civilizations, but their analysis proceeds with the assertion that these are not all that important. As Edward Said observes:

> Certainly neither Huntington nor Lewis has much time to spare for the internal dynamics and plurality of every civilization, or for the fact that the major contest in most modern cultures concerns the definition or interpretation of each culture, or for the unattractive possibility that a great deal of demagogy and downright ignorance is involved in presuming to speak for a whole religion or civilization. No, the West is the West, and Islam Islam. (Said, 2007)

This serves a rather transparent political agenda. As Said maintains:

> In fact, Huntington is an ideologist, someone who wants to make "civilizations" and "identities" into what they are not: shut-down, sealed-off entities that have been purged of the myriad currents and countercurrents that animate human history [. . .] "The Clash of Civilizations" thesis is a gimmick like "The War of the Worlds," better for reinforcing defensive self-pride than for critical understanding of the bewildering interdependence of our time. (Said, 2007)

Our reinvented conceptualization of political culture is meant as an alternative approach to the problem of the relationship between politics and culture that does the work that Said calls for. It's not that culture doesn't matter and that there are no pressing cultural conflicts. As we have seen, the conflicts between the Israeli and the Palestinian narratives are very real and tragic. But there are important alternatives that are built into everyday life. Civilizational conflicts do inform the Palestinian and the Israeli narratives and their connection to the confrontations in everyday practices. A significant view at the checkpoint is that the Israeli is the colonialist. Not only a repressive power, but a power that is the face of Western domination of the legitimate authority of Palestinians, a view held in common by nationalists and Islamists. And for the Israeli, the Palestinians, the Muslims, the Arabs are identified with the barbarism of the East, better controlled militarily. The incompatible specific stories are linked to global challenges. Great civilizations cross, and the conflicts on a small piece of land and the specific challenges of Israelis and Palestinians are on the center stage of global conflict. But this way of understanding the situation reveals only one dimension of daily practices. There are all sorts of resistances and alternatives, as we have observed. Cultures do not only conflict but they also inform each other and the way the conflict and the dialogue between cultures relate to power is very specific.

5

The Power of Culture versus the Culture of Power

We started with our fundamental analytic project, the reinvention of political culture as a concept. Then we turned to our comparative investigation of political cultures being reinvented, and of the resistance to reinvention. In this chapter, I will turn to the internal tension in political cultures, informed by the analysis and the comparative inquiry: the power of culture versus the culture of power. I will then, in the concluding chapter, draw some practical political conclusions concerning the constitution of democratic culture, and the intellectuals' contribution to democratic and undemocratic culture. We move from scholarly inquiry to a consideration of the perennial question, "What is to be done?" Or at least, what should people such as this author and his readers do?

Political cultures are formed and reformed as the power of culture confronts the culture of power. This has been revealed in each of our cases. It is the central struggle in political cultures. The creative grassroots activism of the Central European democratic opposition, the innovative political campaigns of Barack Obama and of the Tea Party movement, and the persistence of Israelis and Palestinians in constituting zones of respectful dignity, each pits the power of culture against the culture of power.

The culture of power has appeared in our inquiry in two forms, as an official truth and as common sense. Around the Soviet bloc, there was an actual truth regime, "truth is already power" as Michel Foucault imagined such a thing, a condition where truth is a manifestation and consequence of power (Foucault, 1984: 75).

There was an official truth. Common sense, in contrast, is a different form of the culture of power, more open to transformation, but also powerfully resistant to change, as we have seen in the American case.

Common sense is less a truth regime, more a prevailing notion of the truth that supports the order of things and is supported by that order. In the Middle East the power of culture confronts common sense about what is possible and desirable, and what is not, as it confronts a truth regime of occupation and terror, where brutal force makes for warring truths.

The power of culture has appeared in our investigations in variety of forms, from the creative autonomous practices of Polish theater and Polish trade unions, to the writing and speeches of Barack Obama and the interpretive and organizational inventiveness of the Tea Party movement, to the struggle to define dignity at an Israeli checkpoint in the occupied West Bank. In each case, the capacity to work with a cultural inheritance and the capacity to create something new presented the possibility to empower alternatives, for the reinvention of political culture.

In the Polish theater and in the Polish trade unions an anti-romantic alternative to the existing order was culturally formed and informed powerful practices that ultimately contributed to the democratic aftermath of the collapse of the Soviet empire. A sober realism, what Adam Michnik called a new evolutionism, what was described by others with the ironic name of a self-limiting revolution, became definitive of the opposition, contrary to the notion of romantic revolt and martyrdom, which is how Poles and others often conceive of Polish political culture. The realistic practices of the Polish alternative culture and alternative social movement became the basis of an Arendtian political power. People met and spoke to each other, acted in each others' presence, and developed the capacity to act together. And as they did this, they also challenged the legitimacy of the party-state. They turned away from the official language, its newspeak, and, in their public transactions, spoke a language free from the rhetoric of Communist ideology. A truth regime was replaced by a free public discourse, which, of course, was not without its problems. A new connection was made between power and language, moving from dogmatic monologue to dialogue.

There was a unified and clearly delineated culture of power, a truth regime. In order to get on with daily life, the official language had to be used, even if it weren't believed. The official language told a simple story that neatly connected past, present, and future, implicating all who used it. Telling different stories, especially in a differently formed language, was a fundamental act of opposition. As the opposition moved from utilizing the official ideology, i.e., the equivalent of the Orwellian "Big Brother is un-good," to developing its own language of opposition in a great variety of different cultural forms, from theater to novels to political manifestos and alternative histories of the recent and not so recent past, the power of the totalitarian state, the legitimation of its authority and its ability to channel the power of concerted social action (i.e., power in the Foucaultian, Weberian, and Arendtian senses) were all frontally challenged. When Solidarity, the political movement in opposition, was repressed in Poland, the development of alternative culture became the central political arena. Given the truth regime, this was not a sublimation of politics in cultural activity, a deferral of real politics. It was the continuation of the main political task that had immediate and lasting practical consequences.

The campaign and presidency of Barack Obama also reveals the power of culture as it confronts the culture of power. Cultural creativity faced an enduring common sense, a distinctively configured democratic culture, that was long ago described and analyzed by Tocqueville, and a creative culture confronted the culture of racism, the grand contradiction of American democratic culture, observed as such by Tocqueville and many other critics.

Tocqueville tried to depict American common sense, a depiction which seems to still apply through time, centered on the ideals of equality and individualism, mediated by a commitment to common goods, realized through voluntary association. But the way these central commitments have been manifested historically has varied in interesting ways, as we have observed. The twentieth century opened with a celebration of the free market (as President Coolidge put it, "the business of America is business"), with skepticism about government involvement in social and political affairs. With Roosevelt and the New Deal, while the market was not attacked, the relationship between state and market was reconfigured. In Tocqueville's terms, simple individualism was balanced by an individualism properly understood. And this broader individualism was realized through government actions. Good government made sense. Left to their own devices, the captains of industry did not have "the average Joe's" interest in mind, while for a large portion of the public, the government, under the stewardship of Roosevelt and the Democratic Party did. Programs and regulations were sensible and necessary, the answer to people's problems. For the most part, the Republican Party worked against this common sense, prevailing in the 1980s with Reaganism. As we have investigated, a major project of Obama has been not only to change free market policies enacted during the Reagan years, but also to change again the balance of the common sense that supported his policies, i.e., government is the problem not the solution. These are related but not identical challenges.

The policies had to change and did. The financial system nearly collapsed, a worldwide economic depression had been a real possibility. Because of this, Republicans and Democrats, along with political leaders of the left and the right across the globe, formulated and developed aggressive government intervention in market activity. Appraising the dimensions of the crisis, the Obama administration went on to "bail out" the American auto industry, and enacted an economic stimulus package to get the economy and the country moving again. The unpopularity of these policies indicated that they have challenged the common sense of a significant portion of the public. The projects were understood as a unified effort at a government takeover, a fundamental threat to American individualism – thus the strange but popular notion that Obama is a socialist. The dimensions of the policy, the size of the programs, made people's heads spin. Deficits were skyrocketing. It appeared to many that the rich and powerful had been helped, along with big banks and Wall Street, while Main Street and small businesses were being ignored. Jobs for ordinary people were not apparently the clear priority. And, as the opposition party is prone to do, the Republican Party blamed all continuing economic problems on the party in power and its leader. It named the attempt to address deep problems in the health-care system as Obamacare, the straw that broke the camel's back, i.e., the public's back. Obama knew during the election that common sense was a key issue. It has proven to be so, although, at least initially, not to his political benefit. But more is involved than the changing fortunes of this or that political figure and political party; the fundamental contours of political culture are at stake.

Obama has attempted to move common sense in one direction, the defenders of the prevailing common sense have pushed back. In both cases, common sense is connected to power, and in both cases the continuity and creativity of culture are involved. Obama has been trying to emphasize the need to link individualism to concern for the common good, while his opponents have been countering with a commitment to the notion that the way to achieve the common good is through individualism. These are old themes in American political culture, one of its central dialogues. The new variations have to do with how they are creatively developed and linked to different kinds of power.

Tea Party activists have done unto the grassroots organizer what he would do unto them. Deprived of the power of the state to enforce their approach to taxation and limited government, as was the case in the Reagan era, they have grounded their power in a very impressive community-based social movement, facilitated by the web and talk radio and cable television, in a way that resembles the Obama campaign, practicing "the politics of small things." Their power is grounded in their capacity to speak and act in each other's presence and to then act in concert in a way that is highly visible to society at large. They draw upon the organizing ideas of the grand old man of community organizing, Sol Alinsky, to oppose his political commitments as they are now being developed by the commander-in-chief, using the full powers of the presidency. Their link to cable news, specifically Fox, and to talk radio, with Rush Limbaugh leading (Chafets, 2010a), makes it so that what the Tea Party activists discuss and do online and in the streets is broadly visible. They are not a majority of the population. They are a distinctive minority – whiter, wealthier, older, more male. They are more conservative and more frequently think that the policies of the Obama administration favor the poor and blacks over whites and the wealthy than the public at large (Zernike and Thee-Brenan, 2010). But nonetheless, despite these limitations and specifications, they have had great impact, in significant ways defining the political agenda. The public at large sees them clearly and must respond. Are they for them or against them? Political candidates ignore them at their peril. They must take a stand, and try to capture the support of the "Tea Party Patriots," a project for Republicans in particular, or directly confront and isolate them, the task for Democrats. In the meanwhile, their creative invocations of the legacies of the Boston Tea Party, and the principles of American constitutional limited government have become an important part of the political scene. Their presence underscores and makes clearly visible the common sense resistance to the changes Obama and his Democratic allies have initiated.[56]

Further, the significance of the Tea Party should not be measured exclusively in terms of electoral politics, in victories and defeats. If one candidate wins because of his affiliation with them (Scott Brown in the special election for the Senate seat in Massachusetts of the late Edward Kennedy), this does not confirm the importance of the Tea Party Movement. And if Tea Party candidates lose elections that otherwise might have been won (Christine O'Donnell in Delaware, Sharon Angle in Arizona, and Carl Paladino in New York), it does not disconfirm the importance. Whether winning or losing, it is because of the movement that the political debate has changed. The common sense of the status quo ante is being defended. Change has been initiated, but its success is not known. The presence and visibility of the Tea Party have played a significant role in defining the American political landscape.

I see a parallel to the anti-war movements of the recent and not so recent pasts here. The anti-war movement that confronted George W. Bush's wars in Afghanistan, Iraq, and "on terror" did not defeat him in the 2004 election. But when the anti-war movement met the Dean campaign, a significant political force was constituted, putting life into the two-party system, culminating in the Obama/Clinton, and the Obama/McCain contests, and the presidency of Barack Obama. The common sense support of President Bush and his war policies that was overwhelming after the attacks of September 11, 2001, was challenged. The anti-war movement during the Vietnam War never really garnered the support of the majority of the population. When the war proponents, including the leading proponent, President Richard Nixon, invoked the notion of a silent majority they were describing a factual reality. But silence and invisibility are not politically consequential, either then or now. That the war was a failure subsequently became the common sense position. The visibility of the Tea Partyers works for the same result for the Obama policies. They indeed are working to "take our country back."

Nonetheless, I think the counter-revolution to the Obama revolution is a rearguard action, a reaction that is not likely to prevail. This is most clearly the case when it comes to the issue of race, where the creative advance of Obama and his supporters is compelling. Obama has demonstrated the importance of cultural creativity in reinventing political culture in the way he has retold the story of the American dream by addressing the American dilemma. Since his speech at the 2004 Democratic Convention, he has re-formulated the dream by emphasizing the diversity of Americans as a key characteristic of American identity, and highlighted his own story as a typically American one: the son of a white mother from Kansas and an African father from Kenya, with a Muslim name, raised for a formative part of his child-hood in Indonesia, and as a teenager by his white grandparents in Hawaii. This story, his story, Obama used to identify with all who did not fit the former typically American mold and to convince those who understood that that mold needed to be expanded. There was beauty and originality in the way he expressed his ideal first in his remarkable memoir *Dreams from My Father*, and then in his many campaign and presidential speeches. The beauty and the originality highlighted a changing American reality, a more diverse society, religiously, ethnically, racially, one in which whites will be a minority in the near future.

The contrast with his opponents could not have been greater.

At the Tea Party demonstrations, the call to take back our country has been a frequent refrain. This is an extension of Sarah Palin's celebration of the real America, "the pro-American America." Although this is not explicitly racist, the nostalgia for the virtues of the small town is no doubt in part a lament for an American society that is no more, a white, Christian America, in which men were men and women were women, and marriage was between a man and a woman, an American America, with people speaking English. This imagined homogeneity was always far from the reality, although it did exist as the norm, the imagined ideal, something which Tocqueville observed as a precondition for the democracy of Anglo Americans (2000: 45–52). Now, even as an ideal, it is something that is passing, and many people are frightened by the prospect. But the fear will not change the reality. And the new imagination, embodied and depicted by Obama, helps a majority feel at home.

On the issue of government involvement in economic affairs and on the question of the place of diversity and the balance between racism and anti-racism, the political culture of the United States has been in flux. There is a battle over common sense. I have a sense that despite the uncertainties, time is on the side of those proposing major changes, but perhaps that is because I am not an uninterested observer. When it comes to matters of race, I think this is likely because of the major demographic changes in American society. When it comes to the political economy, also, the fundamental rationality of the Obama administration's program is likely to lay the groundwork for an economic recovery and then those cultural changes also are likely to prevail. The power of culture would become the new culture of power most clearly with the re-election of President Obama. This would indicate definitive reinvention.

In the case of the Middle East, change is not nearly as likely as it is in the American case, and than it was, in retrospect, in Central Europe (although at the time systemic change seemed to be unimaginable). In Israel–Palestine, the culture of power is most persistent, specifically as the common sense of the two sides of the conflict interact, and as a truth regime of occupation and armed resistance reigns. There is a common sense understanding of the resolution of the conflict, but this is less consequential than it appears to be and is very much in conflict with the common sense positions of the conflicting parties. And common sense combines with truth regime, and they fortify each other, making change even more difficult. The situation is more complicated and it appears to be more enduring than in either the United States or in the former Soviet bloc.

If there is to be a resolution to the conflict, its basic form is known. The details have not all been specified, but the fundamental contours of an agreement have been negotiated by official and unofficial political actors, broadly recognized by political and civil society. A Palestinian state would be established on the West Bank and in Gaza, which would recognize the legitimacy of the Israeli state as the homeland of the Jewish people. Palestinians and Israelis would renounce violent conflict between the sides. Israel would withdraw from the occupied territories back to the 1967 borders with minor negotiated adjustments. The right of Palestinians to return to their former homes would be honored through some combination of symbolic recognition, perhaps including some actual return and compensation for displacement. An expanded Jerusalem would become the capital of both Palestine and Israel. The old city would be internationalized and the rights of the three major religions would be protected. Of course, there are specific problems. Exactly where are the borders to be drawn? How would the right of return be respected? How would the Palestinian state be continuously configured? How would Jerusalem be divided? What is to be done with the Israeli settlements? While one or another of these questions may seem to be an insurmountable obstacle, with a concerted desire to come to an agreement they could be answered. It is the quality of the commitment to an agreement and the trust that it requires that have been lacking. This poor commitment has been an outgrowth of the common sense positions of each side's understanding of self and other.

I should point out that there is another view of a resolution to the conflict that has appeal, especially among a limited group of intellectuals: the bi-national secular state.[57] This has been the official position of the Palestinian nationalists, the PLO, but it also was a minority position among some Zionists during the British mandate. Now it is supported as an alternative on practical grounds, because of the failure of the two-state solution, or on principle, the need to establish a state that is not based on religious and ethnic privilege. This is the position of the Palestinian critics of the peace process, and of anti- and post-Zionists. It is also the nightmare of conventional Zionists, of the left, right, and center, as the demography in Israel, the West Bank, and Gaza points to a Palestinian majority. Given the very strong opposition to this on the part of the vast majority of Israelis, it is not a workable alternative now. Further, the chief Palestinian political movements are opposed, Fatah because it is committed to the two-state solution, and Hamas because it, as an Islamic party, would oppose a secular state. While critics of the two-state solution may find this approach appealing, there is no significant political force that stands behind this idea. This is not to say that the two-state solution really appears viable.

Work toward the two-state solution, the peace process, has continued for more than thirty years, revealing that the commitment may have been more to the process, than to peace. By committing to the process, the leadership on both sides has received political and economic support. By not achieving an agreement, they have avoided the tough struggle to work for its enactment, which would involve serious resistance on the part of significant segments of their constituencies. Among many Israelis, the dismantling of settlements runs against basic norms of the Zionist project. Among many Palestinians, anything short of a clear right of return would be understood as defeat. The stories people tell themselves about themselves and the other would be challenged by a workable agreement.

Thus it is of great importance that different stories are told, key moments when the power of culture confronts the culture of power, of common sense. We have observed people doing this, from Palestinian taxi drivers at the checkpoints to Palestinian cultural and political leaders at Oriental House to the Israeli-

Palestinian Bereaved Families for Peace to Machsom Watch, the Israeli women against the occupation and for human rights at the checkpoints. Not all of the people involved intend to tell different stories, but their actions in small ways constitute alternative large narratives. The politics of small things play an important role in the reinvention of political culture. This is especially the case in Israel-Palestine at this time, while it has been the case at earlier times in the former Soviet bloc and in the United States.

In the not so distant past, in Central Europe, when the end of the Communist system was rarely even imagined, creating small zones of independence, such as the student theater I studied, made all the difference for the people involved. The same pattern was discernible in the black America of the past century, in a broad variety of black associations, from professional groups such as independent media serving the black community, to more explicit political associations such as the Niagara Movement, and to the Southern Christian Leadership Conference. Small zones of independence provided training grounds for major social movements. But more directly, they were places where alternative ways of knowing the world and knowing the relationship between the self and the other were cultivated. This now is the case in Israel-Palestine, as we have observed.

At the checkpoints, Palestinians are subjected to the indignities of the occupation regime. But, at these same checkpoints, they figure out ways to respond creatively to the regime, observe these ways, and discuss their relative merits. One person's resistance, taxi drivers helping people travel through the checkpoint, is another person's collaboration; students who throw rocks at the Israelis but also damage the drivers' cars and trucks. And one person's labeling of another as a collaborator raises questions about class relations and privileges. In everyday interactions unanticipated opportunities are nurtured to establish self-respect and to challenge illegitimate authority, to understand the range of alternative positions and the human challenge in the conflict. Alternative relationships between power and culture are enacted as people negotiate their positions at the checkpoint. The checkpoint is far from being a free space; the coercive power of the occupation officials decides to a significant degree how and when who comes and who goes. But embedded in the comings and goings are the responses of the specific people in the system and their responses change the system and the people in it as a result. The case of Orient House revealed how far this can go. A cultural institution, creatively developed, became a center of national power. Power in the Arendtian sense became power in the Weberian sense, and then power in the Foucaultian sense shut it down. The politics of small things mattered, although it was defeated when the occupation authorities, led by Ariel Sharon, closed Orient House.

But such clear defeat is not permanent and in some sense it was not a defeat at all. Since that time, alternative ways of knowing and alternative powers have developed first at the margins. And because of what was accomplished there and then, the primary definitions of Palestinian resistance and Israeli security have been opened. The common sense remains tragic. What Israelis "know" about themselves and about Palestinians, and what Palestinians know about Israelis and about themselves, do not provide the opportunities for Palestinian and Israeli independence and security and for a resolution of their conflict, even though the contours of the resolution are broadly recognized. But the existence of people who interact in everyday life apart from this common sense, suggests that tragedy is perhaps not the end of the story. Indeed the actions enact the groundwork for different solutions. Because Palestinians and Israelis can call for peace on the basis of their bereavement, it is possible to imagine building the mutual respect that is required to negotiate a two-state solution, where Israelis who remain in the West Bank and Gaza and Palestinians who remain in Israel proper will be accorded minority rights. And indeed because this trust can be established in the relationships among peace activists, but also among Israelis and Palestinians in dealing with practical problems concerning water rights, city planning, health, and education, it is also possible to imagine a secular bi-national state, with full citizen rights of all individuals, a homeland for Jews and Palestinian Christians and Muslims alike. Yet, this potential faces the huge obstacle of very powerful truth regimes.

Indeed, in Israel–Palestine, the struggle over political culture and against common sense is deadly. This is not just a disagreement, or even just a political struggle; in a real sense it is a protracted war that is linked with distinctive ways of knowing, with distinctive truth regimes. As a truth regime, Israelis know about the history of anti-Semitism, a history they understand as being connected to the Palestinian, Islamic, and Arab war against the Jewish state. Each challenge to the legitimacy of Israel, let alone real military and political attacks, is also understood as being a part of this long history, not simply against the interests and security of the nation state. To be against the state is to be anti-Semitic (Gerstenfeld, 2007). Jews who criticize Israel are not real Jews (Cohen, 2010). Advocating a bi-national state is suicidal (Esteron, 2003). This knowledge informs and demands a military response, the occupation. Palestinian knowledge mirrors that of the Israelis, centered specifically around the Nakba. What is the War of Independence for Israelis, is the "Catastrophe" for Palestinians, and all knowledge about self and other revolves around this difference. As George Bisharat put it in his critique of the Geneva Accords, "Like slavery for African-Americans, internment for Japanese-Americans and the Nazi Holocaust for Jews, the "Nakba" ("Catastrophe") was a seminal event in the consciousness of the Palestinian people. No act of the Palestinians justified their expulsion. Their only "crime" was that they were born Christians and Muslims in a place coveted by the Zionist movement for an exclusive Jewish state, and refused to slink off into history as a vanquished people" (Bisharat, 2003). This demands opposition to the Zionist identity by any means. It is such demand that justifies terrorism, the killing of Israelis and their supporters if necessary. Combatants and non-combatants are all complicit, and therefore legitimate targets of self-defense.

Not all Israelis support the brutalities of the occupation and the aggressive military tactics in the wars in Lebanon and Gaza. Nor do all Palestinians support the tactics of terrorism. Indeed, on moral and tactical grounds, it may be that the majority on both sides do not support such actions. Nonetheless, the close connection between these actions and knowledge about self and other help make the action the grounds for perceived truth. The act confirms the idea. The idea is not distinguishable from the act. Knowledge and power become indistinguishable. Ideas can and have been resisted, but they play a hegemonic role. Israelis and even sympathetic supporters of Israel who question war or occupation policies must prove their loyalty, must demonstrate that they are not part of the anti-Semitic hordes. Palestinians who question the tactics of terror must prove that they are really in favor of resistance and not actually collaborators. They do this successfully both on the center stage and in the politics of small things, but the prevailing stories will continue until the time when there are compelling and convincing alternative narratives accepted by the population at large. The continuing peace process that brings neither justice nor peace to any party blocks the emergence of alternative narratives. Palestinians know that all the attempts at person to person reconciliation have not ended the occupation, the settlements, and their economic misery. Israelis know that whenever they offer peace gestures to the other side it is rebuffed, weakening and not strengthening their security. Alternative spaces exist but they have been marginalized by the ongoing conflict.

Thus, in each of our cases, we have seen that power and culture are interrelated, constituting political culture. This is my core conceptual proposal, my attempt to analytically reinvent a frequently used but often abused concept. It has been abused because the concept more often than not has been used exclusively to account for persistence, destiny, while the relationships between power and culture also can be the grounds for change, possibility. Indeed, I have attempted to demonstrate that culture as a creative arena provides the possibility of political alternatives to the order of things, and that the key basis of power can also be changed, contributing to the reinvention of political culture, and opening political cultures to serious contestations. The power of culture confronting the culture of power – the implicit contest in each of our cases – is the central struggle in political cultures. And a key component of this contest can be found in what I call the politics of small things, when changes in gesture and independent association contribute to the reinvention of political culture.

I have proposed a reinvention of a concept to account for the reconfiguration of the relationships between power and culture. This has not been simply an analytic exercise, but a way to make sense of the major issues of our times – the implications and aftermath of the decline and fall of the Soviet empire, the transformation, with perils and promise, of the remaining global superpower, and "the clash of civilizations," as it is manifested in Israel–Palestine. I also hope that this inquiry can inform a deeper understanding of the constitution of democratic culture and the role of the intellectual in supporting such culture, to which I now turn.

6

From Monologue to Dialogue: Democratic Culture and the Intellectuals

Tocqueville and the mid-twentieth-century analysts of political culture were primarily interested in political culture as it supports and is a consequence of democratic practices. Tocqueville believed that there was a vital relationship between democracy as a political system and democracy as a social order with a distinctive culture, as we have observed. Americans with their social practices and "habits of the heart" supported democratic politics and a distinctively democratic culture, and democratic politics and democratic political culture supported Americans in their social practices. Mid-twentieth-century researchers, Almond, Pye, Lipset, et al., were more specific, analyzing comparatively how certain attitudes and beliefs supported democratic institutions and practices, while others undermined them. I think there is a thinness in the social science approach, as demonstrated in chapter 1. But I also think that Tocqueville's analysis is thin, or, more precisely, I think that Tocqueville gets to the fundamental constitution of democratic culture and its major tensions, but only starts the analysis. The implications have to be worked out and they go beyond what the theorists of political culture have presented. At issue is the cultural constitution of a free and dynamic public life. A democratic culture is a culture of publics. This has been apparent in each of our case studies. In the tension between the culture of power and the power of culture, there is a zone for dialogue in democracy, and as I will show in the concluding section of this chapter, intellectuals are key dialogic agents.

When I met Morris Janowitz in his office reporting on the progress of my dissertation research, dialogue as a democratic end in itself was something that he did not appreciate. The fact that the theater movement was neither pro- nor anti-Communist indicated to him that it was politically insignificant. He and many people I spoke to then overlooked the fact that the movement established a social location for free public interactions. This is also something that is not appreciated by those who wonder what the point is of the peace activities of those at the margins of Palestinian and Israeli societies. And it is clearly not recognized by those who underestimated the powerful rhetoric of Barack Obama, and the power of the Tea Party movement in opposition to Obama. For better and for worse, these are manifestations of democratic culture. Each has opened up discussion about pressing issues. Each has moved political culture away from monologue toward dialogue.

When Palestinians confronted an occupation regime at a checkpoint, an embedded potential for dialogue became manifest. There were harsh conflicting monologues articulated here, that existed apart from each other, ignorant of each other: the Palestinian versus the Zionist projects. The Israeli military enacted the occupation regime. Soldiers followed a clear line of command as they did their jobs and a truth regime was constituted. Palestinians were to play their assigned subservient scripts, as they tried to move from here to there. They might attack the regime at the checkpoint and beyond in the name of resistance, but as long as the checkpoint functioned, the truth regime was in place. But more was involved than this. The actions of Israeli human rights groups presented another account of the significance of the actions of soldiers from within the Israeli polity. Their presence stood as a challenge to the truth regime's rendering of the checkpoint. In human rights reports and writings, they questioned the official accounts of military actions and social interactions between Palestinians and Israelis at the checkpoints. The legitimation of the occupation was challenged, as it justified the order of things.

The challenge more directly came from the Palestinian side. Of course, this occurred beyond the immediate situation in the form of political movements and resistance of various sorts, including military engagement. But it was also immediately present, fundamentally directed against the occupation regime but also engaged with it by the way Palestinians moved to and fro. This we saw even in the way working-class taxi drivers responded to the demands of the Israeli authorities as they attempted to make a living, and as middle-class protestors demonstrated against the checkpoint. Alternative positions were enacted and interpreted. People argued about who collaborated and who steadfastly resisted. And such open exchange expanded in various cultural and civil activities.

Such expansion has been a key to the political projects of Barack Obama and his Tea Party opponents. The United States has an open public life, with a well-developed sphere of publics (Gutman and Goldfarb, 2010). There is no systemic closure of public discussion as there is in the Israeli–Palestinian conflict and as there was in the former Soviet bloc. Nonetheless, common sense propositions do prevail and are difficult to transform, and the way political dialogue has appeared has been superficial, conducted in fleeting images and quick sound bytes on television and radio, reported in the printed press, all available on the web. Obama has met these limitations both in form and content, as he has managed to challenge common sense, using serious argument and classical rhetorical eloquence. The Tea Party, subsequently, has managed to respond quite visibly and with significant effect.

As we have seen, Obama is a master of the long form and the deliberate action. In his speeches and actions, as he responds to the crises of the day, he also re-imagines the American dream, by addressing the American dilemma, and he has attempted to move the political center, challenging previously prevailing common-sense propositions about the relationship between the polity and the economy. Yet, I think that in many ways the form of his politics is even more important than this content. The way he has combined the lessons of community organizing, classic rhetorical eloquence, and the new media has suggested new ways to conduct political debate in America and beyond. He opens contemporary politics to serious reflection and intelligence. He battles against emotional reactions, of a politics of fear, and challenges his fellow political leaders and the public at large to work with more difficult emotions, primary among them compassion and intellectual curiosity.

And Tea Partyers have responded, imagining a more homogene-ous vision of what it means to be an American, and proposing and defending a more market-centered set of policies, a more limited form of governance. They make their proposals using the new and old media with sophistication, creativity, and emotional intensity. A new form of more deliberate and sustained politics is confronted by a new form of the politics of small things and media perform-ances of talk radio and cable news. Public discussion is animated, even if it is not always informed.

There is a serious confrontation of alternative positions being presented. But the way they appear highlights the limitations of public discussion in the United States. Major corporations control major media outlets, distorting the news (Chomsky, 1989: 1–12; Debord, 1994: 25–46; Baudrillard, 1988: 166–84). Television amuses, rather than informs the public (Postman, 1986: 92, 130, 140–1). With the emergence of the new media, people consume the news to confirm their biases, leading to atomized publics of prejudice, rather than the public exchange of alternative views (Dayan and Katz, 1992). Instead of serious deliberation about alternative positions concerning problems of the day, there are parallel publics that do not recognize each other. From the point of view of democratic culture in America, these are the worst of times, but also better times.

In Poland and among its neighbors in the eighties, things were simpler. The major media were under the strict control of the party-state apparatus, and there was general agreement among Poles that "television lies," as the signs on the Gdansk shipyards during the strikes that led to the formation of Solidarity in 1980 declared. The public broadcasts and print media that were subjected to the censorship apparatus of the party-state were broadly understood to be systematically distorted. At their best, they had to be read between the lines, and sometimes there was not much there. The alternative media developed in response to this. They developed in direct support of the developing democratic opposition in the seventies, and flourished in the eighties with the ascendancy of Solidarity, first above ground, and then, after martial law, underground. The establishment of free public expression was the great achievement of the opposition. That it was well established before the collapse of the old regime, probably goes a long way in explaining the relative success of democracy in the aftermath of Communism in Poland (Goldfarb, 1992).

The principle of a free public life was a key to this development and a major contribution to Poland's democratic culture. I observed the direct link between the officially accepted but censored cultural expression at the margins in places such as Polish Student Theater, with the development of an autonomous, though illegal, cultural system starting in the mid seventies to Solidarity and the defeat of the Communists in 1989. Among ever-broadening social circles, people could express themselves freely and be heard. They could appear in each other's presence, and even act together. This free public action proved to be the fundamental social and cultural infrastructure of the post-Communist democracy.

But it did have its limitations, the limits of common sense. While many themes that could not be discussed in the official media became open to public debate, such as an objective history of the recent past and the factional history of the Communist Party (the Polish United Workers' Party), other topics, related to popular attitudes and opinions, could not be discussed. It was only after the changes in 1989, that the degree of Polish complicity in the massacre of Jews during the war was opened, and likewise it is only after the changes that the problems of Catholic dogmatism, patriarchy, and homophobia were critically discussed. The openness of public life supported the development of democracy, and the establishment of democracy opened public life.

But this is not just a happy story. An open public life reveals opinions and provides the possibility for public actions that are both heartening and disheartening, that seem to be democratic through and through, and also profoundly anti-democratic. Xenophobia and anti-xenophobia in Poland are an interesting case in point. During the Communist period, public discussions about the Holocaust were minimal and were distorted by official ideology. According to the official script, the Nazis were reactionary and their primary antagonists were the Communists. The struggle was seen as a part of the story of the march to socialism. The virulent, murderous anti-Semitism of the Nazi regime was downplayed – so much so that at the entrance to the museum at the Auschwitz concentration camp, people of all the nations of Europe were commemorated, without mention of the fact that the overwhelming majority of those killed were Jews. Indeed, when I visited the camp in 1973 and 1986, not only were Jews not mentioned in the general description of the camp at its entrance, but the special exhibition to the memory of Jewish victims was closed for repairs and had been for the entire period from 1968 (the year of an anti-Semitic purge in Poland) until 1989. Coming to terms with the history of the Holocaust only began in earnest in Polish society after the collapse of Communism. Until then, official party policy determined what was to be remembered and what was not. More debate about and recognition of Jewish suffering started to appear in the eighties, but this apparently occurred for foreign policy purposes.

But once these things were opened, they proved to be very difficult. On the very positive side, systematic attempts were made to remember and commemorate accurately. The Auschwitz museum was a clear case in point. Also notable were the many signs all around the country marking locations of atrocities. A dedicated group of mostly young people worked hard to remember the victims. On a lighter note, efforts were made to reintroduce Jewish entertainment and popular culture into Polish cultural life. The Jewish Cultural Festival in Kraków was a singular case in point, extremely popular, with broad participation of visitors from abroad and from all over Poland.

Another extremely important positive development was the publication of a very difficult book, *Neighbors,* by the American historian, Jan Gross, which examines a hard reality precisely: "one day, in July 1941, half the population of a small East European town murdered the other half – some 1,600 men, women and children" (2001: xviii). Officially and publicly the Nazis had been blamed for the murders in Jedwabne, but Gross revealed the local knowledge to the contrary. Gross provoked a great national debate in Poland. Many further documented the difficult fact that Poles were not only the victims of Nazi barbarism, but also were complicit in barbarism (Michlic and Polonsky, 2004). But many others, including the head of the Polish Catholic Church, Cardinal Józef Glemp, concertedly impugned Gross's character and motives, and ignored the hard facts that he brought forward.[58]

The same sort of aggression toward those who would challenge common sense is directed toward those who question the sexism of Polish society and its homophobia. As with the case of anti-Semitism, there is the very positive development of new feminist and gay rights voices, and there is also the reactionary attack on these voices, including the revival of censorship (Kitliński and Leszkowicz, n.d.). An open public life is not only a matter of enlightened views: inherited common sense, its critique, and the reaction to the critique are all present. Not every voice is democratic in principle, but the multiplicity of voices contributes to a democratic public life and a democratic political culture, specifically when this multiplicity interacts. Heterogeneous cultural and political tendencies define political culture.

To some degree Tocqueville recognizes this. He is especially sharp on the internal tensions of individualism, which is a strong theme in *Democracy in America,* and which continues to define major competing currents in American political and social life, the tension between a narrow individualism and an individualism with broad horizons, "individualism properly understood." But on other tensions within American culture as a democratic culture, Tocqueville has missed the mark, as we have already observed in chapter 1.

He thought that the tension between the hierarchy that is necessary for the pursuit of cultural excellence with egalitarianism embedded within democracy would result in cultural mediocrity in all sorts of pursuits, and that this would weaken democracy itself, since wise governance would then be elusive. No doubt this was and continues to be a problem, as the calls of the Tea Party movement and the Republican Party's revival of a kind of know-nothing-ism aptly demonstrate. Pretending that the world economic system was not on the brink of collapse did not make the crisis go away. Pressing economic problems cannot be solved by refusing to pay attention to the hard lessons of the great Depression of the 1930s as they apply to the economic challenge of the twenty-first-century financial crisis. Economic knowledge cannot be established by popular prejudice.

This is even clearer in the case of the environmental challenges of the day. A proper assessment of the impact of human activities on climate change cannot be determined by an election or a public opinion poll. There are problems that need to be decided politically, but there are also other problems that cannot be. The scientific consensus concerning the cogency of the theory of evolution should not be decided by the political decisions of scientifically ignorant members of a state review board (McKinley, 2010).

But such effects of democratic ignorance upon cultural judgment have been more the exception than the rule. In general, cultural institutions and the practices of the arts and sciences have developed with an independence from popular judgment and prejudice, informed by democratic insights and sensibilities but not reduced by them; such as was the case of the American literary renaissance that Tocqueville overlooked. Universities, libraries, and museums, major research centers, and elementary schools, as a matter of course have concentrated their efforts on materials and approaches for which the general public has suspicion and, sometimes, even antagonism. Free cultural activity is not nearly as vulnerable in democracies as Tocqueville imagined it would be. The idea that freedom of opinion and expression is most vulnerable in democracies, that conformism is stifling – the judgment of Tocqueville – has been proven to be wrong. There are threats to libraries and schools, universities and research foundations, but these create scandals that indicate that the norm of cultural life is free from censorship and political control. The norm is to protect cultural institutions and practices from popular prejudices. Built into American political culture is both a suspicion of intellectual refinement, indeed anti-intellectualism (Hofstadter, 1963), and protections against this tendency. The presence of both defines our political culture: for example, the great contributions to our public life that come from our great universities, and the suspicion of pointed-headed intellectuals.

This heterogeneous definition of political culture goes beyond such basics, as we have seen. American political culture includes both the culture of racism and anti-racism. Polish political culture includes both anti-Semitism and anti-anti-Semitism. Israeli political culture includes Israeli militarized self-defense and opposition to the excesses of self-defense, as Palestinian political culture includes a great variety of positions on resistance and debates among the resisters as to which form is most effective and ethically justified. Positions may be more or less noble, more or less desirable, but that positions should exist side by side and be debated is fundamental for a democratic public and culture. Open discussion of even reprehensible views constitutes democracy as long as the discussion continues. Fostering discussion and its continuation is a fundamental contribution to democratic culture, while stifling the discussion that still needs to proceed is a fundamental challenge to democratic culture. What happens inside discussions matters as does how one set of discussions is related to another set. And there are public figures who play a special discursive role in this regard, fostering dialogue within public space.

The Intellectuals

I have long been interested in the role of intellectuals in political life. I saw first hand in Central Europe how important they can be in the development of alternatives to the politically and morally unacceptable. In fact, I probably first went to do research in Poland, the defining move of my professional life, because of my sense of how important intellectual dissidents were in that part of the world at that time. Even without viewing the situation in melodramatic terms, even without conceiving dissidents as political heroes fighting against evil totalitarian forces, it was clear that intellectuals were addressing major problems of the geo-political world in ways that challenged people on both sides of the Iron Curtain. People like Andrei Sakharov, Vaclav Havel, and Adam

Michnik challenged easy notions of the free versus the totalitarian world, the socialist versus the capitalist, the progressive versus the regressive. They revealed the power of truth against power. And they understood that abuses of power were not the monopolies of either the capitalist or the Communist. They challenged the order of things in exciting democratic ways. They challenged political clichés.

They challenged me to think differently. I was active in the New Left and the anti-war movement, but I was not happy with their simplicities. Reading about the dissidents in the former Soviet bloc provided a new way of proceeding. But as I read on about the history of intellectuals and specifically the history of intellectuals in East and Central Europe, I realized that intellectuals could just as easily be totalitarian executioners, as their opponents. I read Czesław Miłosz's classic, *The Captive Mind,* and I came to understand how it was that intellectuals could be seduced by totalitarian temptations. And then I read *Humanism and Terror,* by the phenomenologist Maurice Merleau-Ponty, and came to realize that a brilliant philosopher, a great critical intellectual, was capable of developing a strong and direct justification of political horrors, in this case the Stalinist show trials.[59]

During the course of my studies of previously existing socialist societies, I accepted as a given that there were intellectuals on both sides of the barricades, strong supporters of the regime, as well as leading regime critics. It was after the collapse of the previously existing socialist regimes that I felt it was necessary to address a central issue: what distinguished people on one side of the barricade from those on the other. I saw a necessity to highlight the role of intellectuals in supporting and undermining democratic culture because it seemed to me that they were still playing these roles, even as analysts were dismissing them as relics of the past. The way intellectuals went about their tasks was having a great impact in societies aspiring to be democratic and in long-standing democracies, and people were overlooking this with potentially critical consequences. This lead to my book *Civility and Subversion* and it has clear implications for our present investigation of reinventing political culture, specifically democratic culture.

Strangers of a Special Kind

In order to understand the role intellectuals play in supporting and undermining democratic culture, it is necessary to be clear about who the intellectuals are. My working proposition: "The intellectuals are special kinds of strangers, who pay special attention to their critical faculties, who act autonomously of the centers of power and address a general public, playing the specialized role in democratic societies of fostering informed discussion about pressing societal issues" (Goldfarb, 1998: 37).

Intellectuals have a distinctive kind of relationship with their compatriots. They are, in the sense of Georg Simmel (1972), strangers. They are both of the society of which they are part, but also from elsewhere. Simmel's archetypical strangers were tradesmen, and perhaps even more specifically in the European context, Jews. They were both situated in a specific place, but also knew a great deal about the ways of people in places beyond their locality. Intellectuals, it seems to me are a special case in point. They are both in their society, but because of the knowledge of history and life elsewhere, and because of their theoretical knowledge and insights, they are different, "strange." They have something to say to their compatriots, something special to add about the state of affairs because of their special knowledge, but this knowledge can be used for or against democracy. When intellectuals take on a superior stance and attempt to enact their understanding of what needs to be done without public discussion and support, on the basis of their superior knowledge, they undermine democratic culture. They seek to substitute their wisdom for democratically established decisions. When they engage their compatriots and provoke them to talk about difficult issues, so that the issues can then be democratically addressed in a more informed way, intellectuals support democratic culture. They play a democratic role when they open public discussion by *subverting* truth regimes and the restrictions of common sense, and by *civilizing* differences so that those who hold fundamentally opposed positions can speak to each other, opening the possibility that common sense can be more truly in common, taking into account the positions of those who have opposing views.

This is where we, the readers of this text and its author, come in. Such discussion about intellectuals and their democratic role has importance for us. I realize that the label of intellectual is not one that is easily accepted or recognized. For me to call myself an intellectual may seem pretentious, and to call you intellectuals may not appear to be a compliment. But if we ignore the spurious suspicions of elitism, we should recognize that the kind of citizens who read and write books such as this one are the kind of people who are a little different than most of their compatriots when it comes to public affairs, bringing in perspectives from elsewhere, from other times, that makes us a bit strange, but also able to offer different, not necessarily better, views on matters of common concern. Perhaps, indeed, there are more of us than is generally imagined. This is what Gramsci had in mind when he asserted that everyone is potentially an intellectual (Gramsci, 1971: 9). The simple point I am making here is that we, intellectuals, have a role to play in the cultural life of politics, its possibilities of reinvention, the possibility that the power of culture can confront the culture of power in creative and democratic ways. We need also to recognize that the way this power of culture confronts the culture of power can also be quite un-democratic, often anti-democratic. The way we speak to each other and try to speak to specialized and broader publics forms as it informs political culture. Both the form and the content of our engagement are consequential.

It seems to me quite clear that there is nothing enlightened, nothing particularly leftist or rightist, about intellectuals, nothing progressive or reactionary, nothing necessarily good or bad. Certainly there are stereotypes about the critical leftist intellectuals, stereotypes that are promulgated by both critics on the left, for example Edward Said (1994), and the right, for example Paul Hollander (2006). But the situation is more complicated. Were the dissident critics of Communism rightists? Are nationalist and fundamentalist critics of capitalism and its culture leftists? That these questions do not have clear answers reveals that the political orientation of critical intellectuals is far from clear. We intellectuals simply are a type of character that uses the power of culture to take on the problems of the day, including the culture of power, not necessarily for the better, as some self-identified people of the left would have it, nor necessarily for ill, as conservatives sometimes maintain.[60] If we open public exchange about problems, we contribute to formation of a democratic political culture, in the way described in this chapter. If we close public exchange, we move political culture in an undemocratic direction. Indeed, if we actually think that we can answer the question "What is to be done?" in a clear and definitive way, we are part of the problem more than the solution. I saw this in Poland and we can see it in the way that we act these days.

Back then, intellectual dissidents came in two different varieties. There were those who were explicitly anti-Communist, who knew about the evil empire and fought against it in the name of the good society, the West, Christian civilization, against atheistic Communism. They were more nationalist than their competitors, thought of themselves as the real Poles, and were disparaged as such by their opponents. They knew what needed to follow Communism, as they identified with the glories of the Polish past and an imagined Polish future. They tended to be closer to the Church hierarchy.

There were others who abstained from a vigorous anti-Communism. They often had leftist backgrounds. Many either were themselves once members of the party or they were children of Communists of significant standing. They were closer to elite artistic and academic circles. They had complicated relations with the Church, including often a personal history connected to anti-clericalism and a connection with liberal theologians. Skepticism, rather than belief, was a central part of their intellectual orientation, irony, rather than earnestness, their prevailing attitude.

Both groups were in the opposition movement, both groups supported Solidarity, both played roles in the post-Solidarity, post-Communist period, with the "real Poles" being less visible before the fall of Communism, their opponents less visible after the fall. In the opposition, in notes written in the underground, the question of "What is to be done?" was frequently posed by both sides (Bernhard and Szlajfer, 1995). And representatives of each group had simple answers, though after the changes these simple answers multiplied. For the first group, the answer was Poland. For the second group, the answer was democracy. For both groups, at least initially, these first answers were equated with a second, capitalism, with its free market.

I am simplifying here. But I do so to make a clear point. Both answers, as complete answers, did not serve democratic culture. Intellectuals who held to these positions served the development of a democratic political culture not when they answered the question but when they helped others answer it. If they presented their positions to provoke discussion and responded to each other, they furthered the development of democratic culture. Thus one of the great moments in the development of opposition intellectual life was the underground publication of Adam Michnik's *The Church and the Left,* a book that indeed imagined and provoked such a discussion.

After the collapse of the Soviet order, all sorts of intellectuals, foreign and domestic, moved to assist what was then popularly called the transition to democracy (O'Donnell et al., 1986). Economists would provide advice on shock therapy (Sachs, 2005). Legal scholars would present blueprints on constitution making and reform (Scheppele, 2005). There was a great political debate over whether the state or the economy had primacy, or whether the key engine of transition is civil society. One thing seemed to be agreed upon by just about all the policy analysts: the intellectuals, the independent generalist critics such as Michnik, were no longer needed. Their lack of professional expertise assigned them to the anti-Communist past, if not to the dustbin of history (Mokrzycki, 1996).

There was something compelling and convincing about this common agreement, even as the experts disagreed among themselves about what practical reform, which policy advice, should be followed and in what sequence. Intellectuals in the opposition social movement had an important role to play. They had to morally lead. They had to bravely speak truth to power. They had to help society at large to see that such speech was possible for themselves and for others. But with the transition, such moral leadership and talk were no longer needed. Such talk was seen to be frivolous. It was cheap, did not have real value, when practical reforms were pressing.

Yet, there was a significant problem with this critique of intellectuals. It overlooked some basic elements of power and of culture, of political culture, as should be clear from our inquiry. In order for practical programs to work, they needed to have legitimacy. They needed to be supported by people in their concerted actions in order to be democratic. A truth regime could be established by experts, but a democratic culture requires the discussion that intellectuals, that "dying class," were particularly able to provide. Public support is necessary, and intellectuals can engage the public so that its support would be forthcoming. When things seem to be going wrong, when they seem to be falling apart, we can challenge common sense, in a hope that sound plans can be enacted. When there is significant conflict, through civil engagement, we can hope to make it so that enemies become opponents, and opponents find ways that they can work together. The rocky post-Communist road required such engagement, and it is just as necessary in established democracies, such as the United States, and in settings of profound conflict, such as Israel–Palestine. We have things to do, even when we do not know precisely what is to be done.

Intellectuals and Democratic Culture in the United States and Beyond

In the United States, as a political leader and his political supporters are reinventing a political culture, and as their opponents are opposing reinvention, intellectual civility and subversion are of great importance. The pressing challenge for us as intellectuals is less a matter of choosing a side and prevailing, more about challenging the prevailing political clichés and making it possible for people with opposing positions to make sense of each other and develop a capacity to act together, opening up public life. We should civilize differences and subvert the common sense that hides problems from inspection and possible resolution. I stand by my general position.

Yet, there is a special problem in the present political and media environment. While there are serious and reasonable political conflicts, the daily political spectacle quite often hides rather than reveals the issues of our times. The confrontations about the pressing problems of the day are clouded by media performances that conceal more than they reveal, that often involve a flight from political responsibility and indeed from empirical reality. The political contest is real, specifically concerning the fundamental shape and direction of the political economy and concerning the nature of American identity, as we have seen in chapter 3. But the debate over these issues is hidden by public performances that entertain, engage, and inspire (not bad things at all), but also often intentionally and unintentionally misinform.[61] There are real issues that should be debated, but more often than not instead of informed debate, there are the wild performances of talk radio, cable television news, and the blogosphere, where ranting for the already convinced replaces persuasion, and facts are optional conveniences. As Obama has introduced a new seriousness to public discourse, fighting against sound bytes, the masters of sound bytes and provocative performances are fighting back. The Republican opposition to Obama and the Democrats seems to be guiding these performances. Entertaining and outrageous talking heads, such as Rush Limbaugh and Glenn Beck, have become in a real sense leaders of the opposition, defining the debate (Chafets, 2010b; Kakutani, 2010).

I want to be realistic about this. I know that politics is not and should not be reserved for the highly refined and highly rational. Politics is not an ideal speech community and more is involved in politics than the exchange of rational arguments and the presentation of empirical evidence (Gutman and Goldfarb, 2010). It is and should be about persuasion and mobilization by a variety of different means. Too many people would be excluded if highly rational deliberations defined political debate and contest in democratic life. Democratic politics must be an inclusive enterprise. But when entertaining spectacle and a casual relationship to factual truth become norms of political exchange, a primary responsibility for us as intellectuals is to fight these trends. The challenge today is to demonstrate how this fight is not a partisan position, given the commitment of each side to its rhetoric.

Partisan as I am, I cringe when I hear Republicans describe "the bank bailout" (the Troubled Asset Relief Program), the stimulus package and health-care reform as part of a whole, as unnecessary, budget-busting, expansions of government, and, further, as evidence that Obama and the Democrats are socialists. I think that these characterizations are simply not true. Nonetheless, I realize that there is a view of the world that could lead to such interpretation, at least as an ideological call to action, in the sense of Clifford Geertz (1977). Though I disagree with this position, I know for some it makes sense. While there is a broad consensus among economists that the rescue of large financial institutions was necessary to avoid a global financial crisis, followed by a global economic depression, political actors can judge to the contrary that the inner workings of the market would have corrected the situation on their own. Thus the bailout was an inappropriate intervention. While there is also a consensus among economists that the stimulus package has softened the effects of the recession (the degree of success is a matter of debate), there are those who cogently think it has made matters worse, and that it therefore was little more than a political handout to special interests. And the same people are convinced that more market and less government would control the escalation of medical expenses, making medical care available to the American public and controlling the federal deficit.[62]

I strongly disagree with these judgments, but they are a matter of debate. I know that intellectuals in a democracy need to encourage this debate, make judgments, and take part in the debate. In the noise of the daily political spectacle, though, we have a responsibility to reveal what is at stake, to separate the ridiculous from the challenging. We need to make clear that neither side is treasonous, that the country has not been taken over by an alien without clear citizenship, that the establishment of socialism is not a done deal and fascism is not around the corner, even as we recognize that there is a great deal on the line. Conversely, we need to demonstrate that not everyone that opposes Obama's programs is a racist. We have the same responsibilities as our fellow citizens to make political judgments and to act upon these, but we also have the responsibility to illuminate, to separate sense from nonsense.

Here I think there are special problems. So much of the opposition to Obama is nonsensical that separating sense from nonsense appears as partisan. The pressing challenges in American political culture involve partisan position and a struggle to be sensible. Obama is a stellar figure on both scores. While he has pursued his own projects, which are sometimes provocative for his opponents, he has also worked to do so in ways that are quite sensible. His opposition has formulated their alternatives in unreasonable ways. Intellectuals should be on both sides of the partisan divide, and they are. They should civilize disagreements and attempt to disrupt the complacencies of common sense, and they do. But we all should be against nonsense. Unfortunately, this is not the case. When I think about what needs to be done for the good of American democratic political culture, to what we intellectuals should commit ourselves, I think the battle against nonsense should be the first item on our agenda.

Reinventing political culture involves changing the culture and its relationship with power, relating cultural creativity and not only cultural inheritance to power, of a variety of different sorts. This relationship is democratic when open public discussion exists between culture and power. Intellectuals should work on this discussion, open it and sustain it by encouraging the discussants to take into account the problems of the day, and as we have seen here, to seek to be truthful about those problems. The importance of this is most evident when we in the United States, and in the West more generally, look abroad, especially when we look at a small piece of land on the eastern edge of the Mediterranean, Israel–Palestine. This has become the tinderbox of world affairs, a place of intense importance to great civilizations, where their purported clash is most apparent. We have seen that sometimes such appearances hide more elemental realities. Instead of civilizational clashes, there are many different heterogeneous interactions that follow and undermine the big conflicts. And as I look at this situation, it is clear to me what needs to be done, and it is directly related to what got me into this business in the first place, the intellectual figures of dissidents in the former Soviet bloc.

In Israel–Palestine, there is a need to highlight the role critical intellectuals can play, along with their compatriots, at presenting alternatives. Not because such alternatives are inevitable or even likely, but because they present overlooked possibilities. As intellectuals in the West try to make sense of the Israeli–Palestinian conflict, that possibilities are overlooked is apparent. Not only is there an impasse between the occupiers and the occupied at checkpoints, and at the internal and international borders, there is also an impasse between political leaders and citizens and non-citizens that is more or less ambiguous. Outsiders, looking in, and insiders, looking out, intellectuals as strangers of all sorts, also are at an impasse. I will conclude by examining how some intellectuals on the ground help to overcome the impasse, drawing upon the findings of our inquiry. They provide visions of overcoming the limits of inherited political culture, showing how political culture can be reinvented, as the power of culture confronts the culture of power. A sober assessment of the Israeli–Palestinian conflicts highlights the impossibility of the situation. The ways the sides view themselves and others underscores tragedy, as we have observed in chapter 4. As we also saw, there are alternatives on the ground. I think this opens up a possibility for intellectual action that is generally overlooked and exemplifies what I think the distinctive role of intellectuals is in the reinvention of political culture. I think it suggests not only why civility and subversion are generally superior to more tendentious approaches in supporting the constitution of democratic culture. It also suggests why it is likely that it will be more consequential.

Strong partisan positions on the conflict are common enough, and intellectuals should and do take part. There are those who steadfastly defend and promote one side, and criticize and diminish the other, who defend the Israeli government's actions, or the positions of its parliamentary opposition, and criticize their opponents. There are those who defend the policies of Hamas or Fatah, and criticize their opponents. There are those who explore possible solutions to the conflict, promoting peaceful or military solutions, critically evaluating alternatives. And, there are others whose work is motivated by an attempt to understand their own side, by understanding empathetically the position of the other. I find the last group most interesting, of real intellectual stature, heroes of civility and subversion. I have found particularly enlightening the writing and the activities of Edward Said, Amos Oz, Raja Shehadeh, David Shulman, and David Grossman. As a group, they remind me of the East European intellectuals that I first knew from afar when I was becoming interested in the politics and culture of the former Soviet Union and its bloc, many of whom I later came to know personally. They ask uncomfortable questions. They don't follow the logic of the major power centers in their society, and they work at understanding their counterparts on the other side of the conflict, exploring resolutions without abandoning their primary commitments. Their activities and writings can seem naïve and unrealistic, but their idealism is actually a cogent form of realism. They take into account the human facts on the ground, existing apart from the ideological renderings of those facts. I admire such works especially as they provide alternatives to the ideological debate about the situation. They highlight the specific activities that initiate the reinvention of political cultures.

While others argue with more or less cogency about the fundamental pathology of the Zionists or the anti-Zionists, of the Islamists and nationalists, or the anti-Islamists or anti-nationalists, David Shulman has dissented in the occupied territories week after week. He went not as a distinguished scholar (of the languages and culture of India), but as an Israeli citizen, an activist in the Arab–Jewish Partnership, *Ta 'ayush*, an organization of volunteers established in the first days of the Al-Aqsa Intifada, the Second Intifada. Shulman sought understanding and peace with his Palestinian counterparts as he in his organization attempted to help those who suffer from the consequences of the occupation of the West Bank and Gaza. In *Dark Hope: Working for Peace in Israel and Palestine*, he modestly chronicles his activism. He reveals a difficult situation. He and his fellow Jewish Israelis are from the occupying tribe. The Palestinians are the occupied, or those who have uncertain, second-class Israeli status, subjected to skepticism from other Palestinians and Jewish Israelis. Military force, much of it far from justified, is used in his name. Resistance, much of which is not commendable, is exercised in the name of the Palestinians. He focuses on the problems of his own tribe, anticipates that his Palestinian colleagues will focus on theirs.

At the demonstrations, Shulman works carefully on his presentation of self, on his demeanor, not wanting to appear arrogant. He speaks whenever possible in what this accomplished linguist calls his imperfect Arabic, so he can speak with his Palestinian neighbors with due deference. He, and his fellow Israeli activists and Palestinian activists, work to define themselves as equals, offering mutual respect, dedicated to the problems at hand, protesting the mistreatment by settlers of Palestinian cave dwellers in the hills of Hebron, the injustices directed toward the Palestinian residents of East Jerusalem, forced transfers, demolition of housing and the like, and the tough struggles all over the West Bank, bringing food to the hungry, supporting those who peacefully protest the many abuses of the occupation regime. The group's activities started with food and continued with a broad variety of demonstrations, but given the difficult situation during the intifada, they continually returned to food.

The activists carefully and respectfully listened and responded to each others' concrete practical situation, knowing that they can only get to an understanding and work together by doing so. Neither side understood the situation accurately without taking into account the perceptions and concerns, dilemmas and obligations of the other. They, in a sense, enact the settlement of the conflict in the moment of their common action based on understandings that go beyond the prevailing narratives, the opposing common understandings: the Zionist and the anti-Zionist, the Palestinian nationalist and Islamic, and the anti-Palestinian, anti-Arab, anti-Islamic. They do not, of course, establish the solution, but in the situation of common action, they develop a working one with their bodily actions, challenging the prevailing cultural understandings, the common sense that fuels tragedy.

This is not easy beyond the situation of common action, as David Grossman's life experience reveals. He has written eloquently about the experience of the cave dwellers and has written major works exploring Palestinian–Israeli relations. As Shulman dissented with his body, Grossman wrote a public letter to a Palestinian friend during the Second Intifada, soon after the brutal stabbing of two Israeli reservists on October 12, 2000, who apparently lost their way, just outside of Ramallah. Grossman's friend in Ramallah, with whom he usually speaks during and after crises, had been silent after the stabbings. Grossman imagines in his public letter their first private conversation after the killings, as therapy for himself and to make his political points. In his letter, he works to understand the conflict through Palestinian eyes, but of course it is he who is doing the imagining, and he uses this understanding to account for his own position. He is trying to tell the story of the common sense challenges that Shulman and his colleagues enact. Grossman criticizes the political leaders on both sides of the conflict, and depicts the tragic suffering and death of innocents on both sides. He closes with an appeal for continued conversation, but he included a sense of the torment that exists between two fathers who are friends on opposing sides of the conflict:

> You know when I watch the television broadcasts, I always try to watch through your eyes. I see a Palestinian throng storming an Israeli Army position, and I try to single out a single face, which might be the face of one of your children. I know that you don't approve of this type of demonstration, that it is foreign to your character as one who opposes all forms of violence. But perhaps under these new circumstances it is hard to control a teenage boy who was but a toddler at the time of the first intifada. Perhaps he has grown up on the proud heroic stories of teenage boys of that time and longs to be part of his people's resolute violent struggle for independence. I gaze at the photographs and I see how the hands are raised, holding stones. I see how the faces are contorted with hatred. I see the Israeli soldiers taking aim and shooting and I think of my own son, who will soon enlist in the army. Will his face and body also adjust to those attitudes of war and hatred? (Grossman, 2004)

In 2008, days after he publicly urged his government to accept a ceasefire, Grossman's son, Uri, died in the war in Lebanon, killed by a Hezbollah anti-tank missile. As he spoke about Uri in his eulogy, Grossman revealed a pride in his service, but also a pride in Uri's capacity "to be truly sensitive to the suffering of the other, even if that other is your enemy on the battlefield" (Grossman, 2006). Grossman has ideas about what should be done, but his contribution lies more directly in his concern to recognize the humanity of the self and other on both sides of the conflict. The bitter irony of Grossman's life is that he himself has become a victim of the tragedy that he has highlighted and attempted to address in his writing in such masterly non-fiction books as *The Yellow Wind, Sleeping on a Wire,* and *Death as a Way of Life.*

While both Grossman and Shulman work from committed experience to express their Israeli dissent, Raja Shehadeh has published diaries that have poetically documented the experience and its connection to the struggle for human rights from a Palestinian point of view. He is a founder of the Al-Haq, the pre-eminent Palestinian human rights organization. In his diaries, he documents how those rights have been abused, very much connected to his own everyday experiences, and shows how they lead to a course of action which is grounded in the respect for individual dignity. Grossman, Shulman, and Shehadeh in a sense speak the same language. They are careful in their respect for individual distinctiveness, and they tend to shy away from complete political solutions to complex human problems. In Shehadeh's case, this is grounded in his complex relationship with his highly politicized father, a man who was a "premature" advocate of a two-state solution, who may have paid for his politics with his life. The mystery surrounding the circumstances of his murder is one of the subplots that drives the poetry of Shehadeh's coming of age memoir *Stranger in the House.*

Edward Said and Shehadeh were political collaborators. Said, the world-renowned Palestinian American critic of American and Western approaches to the Middle East and beyond, was a self-reflective and self-identified intellectual. He accounted for this status by speaking truth to power and his status as an exile (Said, 1994). He was a relentless anti-Zionist, from the beginning to the end of his career as a public intellectual. But, he was a critical anti-Zionist, as capable of criticizing the Palestinian powers, as he was a resolute critic of the Israeli state and its policies. He looked closely and paid attention to the details of Palestinian life and suffering. And when he criticized the inadequacies of the Palestinian leadership, he sought alternatives on the ground, which were responding to the lived experiences of Palestinians, very much the experiences illuminated by Shehadeh in his observations of Palestinian society under occupation. In 2002, as the intifada was accomplishing little, Said, along with a number of other prominent Palestinian intellectuals, including Shehadeh, under the leadership of Dr. Mustafa Barghouti, were looking for a third way, an alternative to Fatah and Hamas (Said, 2002). In an essay inspired by a speech he heard given by Nelson Mandela, then a retired, elder statesman, Said described what he saw as the only alternative, "What we never concentrated on enough was that to counteract Zionist exclusivism, we would have to provide a solution to the conflict that in Mandela's second phrase, would assert our common humanity as Jews and Arabs ... we did not focus enough on ending the military occupation as a moral imperative or on providing a form of their security and self determination that did not abrogate ours" (Said, 2005: 50–1). Change "Zionist" to "anti-Zionist" in this quote and it could have been easily written by Grossman or Shulman.

Shulman and Grossman, Said and Shehadeh, and the sensibilities and judgments they represent, have not and will not agree in the way they interpret flashpoints of the conflict. The wars in Gaza, Lebanon, one-state or two-state solutions, on such issues such people do conflict. Ultimately they stand on opposing sides of the conflict. What outrages Grossman and Shehadeh during the intifada is different. But the recognition of the humanity of the other binds them to a similar intellectual project. Being from elsewhere, being knowledgeable about past conflicts and knowing each other, they can think about experience and imagine a different reality that takes into account the situation of common humanity. They open up space for a discussion of that humanity, and thus can imagine not only a possible resolution to the conflict, but a possibility that the resolution might be democratic. In politics means are ends, an Arendtian point that we have returned to throughout our exploration. These conflicting intellectuals demonstrate this as they pursue their specific interests, reflecting upon lived experiences of people locked in tragedy. They are opposition intellectuals, trying to lay the groundwork for alternatives to the tragedy in which they are embedded.

Postscript

My friends in Poland and around the old bloc acted as if they lived in a free society, and in the process they laid the groundwork for perhaps the most positive peaceful change of the twentieth century. Barack Obama retold the American story and recreated the field of American political culture, opening new promise but also revealing new perils. Israeli and Palestinian intellectuals retell the stories of their respective tribes seeking to connect the retelling to power, as people in their everyday lives constitute ways to establish dignity and respect, and work on understanding. From Poland to the United States to Israel–Palestine when the power of culture confronts the culture of power, political culture can be and has been reinvented, changing the basis of power and changing power's relationship to culture, distancing the power of the party-state from culture and the power of concerted action in East Central Europe, using the power of political rhetoric to challenge American common sense on issues concerning the relationship between capitalism and democracy and on questions of race and American identity, being developed by ordinary people and a group of prominent but politically marginal intellectuals, who work with and against each trying to go beyond tragedy in Israel–Palestine. Political culture is developed, and it matters, providing the grounds for alternative futures. The reinvention of the concept of political culture is a theoretical necessity, enabling us to better understand how our political world works. It is also an intellectual imperative, as we try to not only understand the world, but also to democratically change it.

Notes

1 I have worked on this in much of my writings, including *The Persistence of Freedom, On Cultural Freedom, Beyond Glasnost, After the Fall, Civility and Subversion*, and *The Politics of Small Things*.
2 Cultural transformation as a precondition for systemic change is the subject of my book *Beyond Glasnost*.
3 Janowitz's major work was his *The Professional Soldier: A Social and Political Portrait*. For a representative sampling of his sociology see Janowitz and Burk, 1991.
4 For a sense of the group see their website, www.theparentscircle.com/
5 Avni, Ronit (Director./Producer/ executive Producer), *Encounter Point*, Just Vision, 2006. See their website, www.encounterpoint.com/about/index.php.
6 The classical post-war literature on the topic includes: Pye and Verba, 1965; Verba and Nie, 1972; Pye, 1972; Almond and Verba, 1989; Lipset, 1990.
7 We will focus on Putnam, 2000, and Eliasoph, 1998.
8 See the next section of this chapter.
9 See also other works by Fine and associates that contribute to an examination of this location for the constitution of political culture: Fine, 1979, 1989, 1991, 1998, 2000; Fine and Holyfield, 1996; Fine and Kleinman, 1979; Fine and Stoecker, 1985; Fine, Hallett and Sauder, 2004.
10 I analyze this in *Beyond Glasnost*.
11 This theme is intensively analyzed in Jones, 2009.
12 For an extended Foucaultian analysis of the Israeli–Arab relations, see Eyal, 2008.
13 This was the position of both radical and conventional sociologists. See Gouldner, 1980, and Parsons, 1971.
14 For two very different overviews see Anderson, 1976, and Kołakowski, 1978 (especially vol. III).
15 For an overview in historical context see Judt, 2006.
16 For a contemporary account see Lewis, 1958.

17 For contemporary accounts see Feher, 1979, and Vajda, 1979.

18 I analyze the role of Moczar in *The Persistence of Freedom*.

19 This explanation was developed by Georg Lukacs (1971), the great Marxist cultural critic.

20 I attended a National Endowment for the Humanities in the summer of 1981. During the course of this seminar this judgment of the contemporary Soviet theater was the common judgment of the participants.

21 For novels, see Konrad, 1974; Kundera, 1980, 1984; Hrabal, 1990a, 1990b; Kis, 1990; Konwicki, 1982, 1983; Andrzejewski, 1997; Borowski, 1992.

22 Gomułka in 1970.

23 This is most readily accessible in the issues of the *Polish Sociological Bulletin*.

24 I consider this transformation of the totalitarian imagination in *The Politics of Small Things*.

25 For colored revolutions see Kuzio, 2007; for cedar revolution see Morley, 2005; for Iran revolution see Black, 2009.

26 The notion of hegemony as Gramsci developed in his prison notebooks and as it has been broadly picked up is often used to name what I am calling common sense. I question the connection of culture to class of this interpretive tradition, so use common sense instead. To be precise, while I do question the necessary connection to class, I recognize the empirical connection is often there. See Gramsci, 1971.

27 I first developed this criticism in *The Politics of Small Things* (Goldfarb, 2006). I wanted to make clear that Foucault cannot distinguish between modern liberalism and modern tyranny (totalitarianism) and highlighted the significance of this. I want to be clear, though, that by identifying this problem, I am not dismissing Foucault's position, but rather pointing to a specific limitation, facilitating what I hope is a fruitful delimited application of Foucault's approach.

28 He made these remarks in an interview given to the editorial board of the *Reno Gazette Journal*. Reported in Murray, 2008.

29 See Katznelson, 2006, for an analysis of how racism was embedded in the actual practices of the New Deal.

30 The kind of appeal Palin is making is linked to a long tradition in American political culture. For a thorough analysis see Shulman, 2008.

31 In a 2009 survey, 52% agreed there is "a lot of discrimination" against Hispanics; 49% agreed when asked the same question about blacks; 58% when asked about Muslims (Pew Research Center for the People and the Press, 2009).

32 Specifically the Tea Party Movement.

33 On the Simpson Case and response see further, www.law.umkc.edu/faculty/projects/ftrials/simpson/simpson.htm.

34 He was returning from China where he was filming the ancestral home of the great American cellist Yo Yo Ma. *Faces of America with Henry Louis*

Gates, Jr. premiered nationally Wednesdays, February 10–March 3, 2010 on PBS.

35 Henry Louis Gates Jr. is perhaps the most widely recognized African American scholar in America. Mr. Gates is also a one-man intellectual and media conglomerate: a co-founder of the genealogy website AfricanDNA. com and the director of the W. E. B. Du Bois Institute for African and African American Research at Harvard; editor-in-chief of the website Oxford African American Studies Center; editor-in-chief of The Root, a website on African-American news, culture, and genealogy. He co-edited the eight-volume *African American Biography* (Gates and Higginbotham, 2008); the five-volume *Africana: The Encyclopedia of the African and African American Experience* (Appiah and Gates, 2005); and *Finding Oprah's Roots, Finding Your Own* (Gates, 2007).

36 In Research 2000 for *Daily Kos* it was reported that 58% of Republicans either did not believe that Obama was a citizen (28%) or were not sure (30%). See Kos, 2009.

37 Compared by Garry Wills to Lincoln's famous Cooper Union Speech (Wills, 2008).

38 There was in fact a considerable distance between what happened at these debates and how they appeared in the media. The sensational and confrontational were highlighted. They made good TV, radio, and copy. See Dionne, 2009.

39 See Freedom Works tactical guide for the August recess: www.freedom-works.org/publications/august-recess-town-hall-meetings, accessed August 26, 2009.

40 Thus, in this chapter, my quotes from his speeches are rather long. He doesn't communicate through short phrases, but through well-developed arguments and images.

41 I analyzed this in Goldfarb, 1991.

42 For Clinton's comparison see http://blogs.abcnews.com/politicalpunch/2008/01/bubba-obama-is.html; for Obama's remarks see www.huffington post.com/mayhill-fowler/obama-no-surprise-that-ha_b_96188.html; and for McCain's economic appraisal see www.huffingtonpost.com/2008/09/15/mccain-fundamentals-of-th_n_126445.html.

43 For my close analysis of that speech, drawing upon the approach to American political culture developed here, see www.deliberatelyconsidered.com/2011/01/with-the-presidents-state-of-the-union-soon-a-look-back-to-a-2008–speech-about-race/, accessed January 16, 2011.

44 As this book goes to press, he did this in a remarkable way in his speech at the Memorial Service for the Victims of the Shooting in Tucson, Arizona, successfully working on his centrist project of redirecting the American common sense. See www.deliberatelyconsidered.com/category/topics-barack-obama/, accessed January 16, 2011.

45 In *The Politics of Small Things,* I posit the idea that the web is the distinctive tool of the left, while talk radio and also Fox are the weapons of the right. I think that this still stands. What is unique here is that these media have facilitated the development of a participatory social movement.

46 This is the general problem that faced the Labor Party and which was experienced by Yossi Beilin specifically.

47 The following discussion on the checkpoint is an interpretation of the careful fieldwork of Rema Hammami (2005).

48 The framework for understanding micropolitics presented in this chapter draws upon major works of Foucault, de Certeau, Mead, Goffman, and Arendt. I have used here: Foucault, 1973, 1979; Rabinow, 1984; Burchell, Gordon, and Miller, 1991; Certeau, 1984; Mead, 1963; Goffman, 1959, 1967; Arendt, 1958, 1961, 1968. Mead's work specifically provides a way to understand Weber's notion of legitimate power in an interactive context. Goffman does the same for Arendt, and of course Foucault speaks for himself.

49 A women's peace organization, Machsom Watch, regularly monitors the interactions at the checkpoints. Their reports are used here for the depiction of the checkpoint world of interaction. See www.machsomwatch.org/en. I am also drawing on the memoir of an Israeli peace activist (Shulman, 2007).

50 I systematically develop this theme as it appeared in Central Europe in Goldfarb, 1989.

51 See www.orienthouse.org/about/history.html, accessed October 28, 2007.

52 Faisal al-Hussaini is the son of Abd al-Qadir al-Hussaini, who lost his life in 1948 defending Jerusalem. His death became a symbol in the Palestinian history.

53 Thomas first presented his idea about the definition of the situation in his *The Unadjusted Girl* (1923).

54 This is beautifully described by Shulman (2007).

55 I analyze this intensively in *Beyond Glasnost* and in *After the Fall.*

56 I want to emphasize the interesting interplay between power and culture here. The long view suggests that Obama and his supporters are creatively reinventing the culture and linking to a new approach to politics, but as they are connected to official power, the Tea Party's retelling of the American story of limited government and of the events of the Tea Party is a kind of reinvention, which would sustain tradition as they see it. The power of culture confronts the culture of power on both sides.

57 See as a prime example Judt, 2003.

58 Glemp gave an interview in the Polish Catholic News Service (KAI). It was full of explicit anti-Semitism. Polish-Jewish conflicts in the thirties had no religious basis, according to the Cardinal. Asked if he thought that Jews experienced a rise in attacks during Holy Week because of accusations of God-killing, as reported by Gross, the Cardinal expressed astonishment.

"This statement strikes me as improbable. The first time I ever heard of this rise in anti-Jewish feeling was in Mr. Gross's book. Clearly the book was written 'on commission' for someone." Glemp, the most senior Polish cleric, all but accused Gross of being in the pay of the Zionists, or the international Jewish conspiracy, or is it the Jewish lobby, or perhaps even "The Elders of Zion?" The Cardinal went on: "Polish-Jewish conflicts did occur in those times (in the thirties), but they had an economic basis. Jews were cleverer, and they knew how to take advantage of Poles." Arguing for the exhumation of the site of the atrocities, contrary to a request by Jews to honor religious law and refrain from desecrating the graves, he defended his position by asserting "Jewish law is not binding in Poland," as if that were the issue, not realizing that it is a matter of honoring and respecting customs other than your own, so that you may honor and respect people whom you don't consider to be of your own. He wanted to do this "because it is important to know the number of victims." Glemp and many respected Polish academics and scholars thought this a central issue. The number of victims is an issue of great moral and political importance, but it does not change the moral challenge if "only" 400 people, "Jews," were brutally murdered by their neighbors, "Poles," instead of 1,600. Glemp went on, wondering why Jews slander Poland, "when Jews had it relatively the best with us, here in Poland." And further: "We wonder whether Jews should not acknowledge that they have a burden of responsibility in regard to Poles, in particular for the period of close cooperation with the Bolsheviks, for complicity in deportations to Siberia, for sending Poles to jails, for the degradation of many of their fellow citizens, etc." In his reflections on Jewish cleverness, there are the Jewish banker and lawyer, the capitalists. In his reflections on the Soviet occupation, there are the Jewish Communists.

But in the reaction to the Jebwabne revelations, there is also much that is worse than is revealed in the Cardinal's interview, with vile and more aggressive anti-Semitism, and this is given support by the manifestly less pernicious and refined refusal to face the legacies of the past. It opened a space for refined and vulgar anti-Semitism. There are those who worry about the numbers, who think the evidence of the murder is still not in. There are those who ask, "Is the hubbub surrounding Jebwabne intended to eclipse the responsibility of Jews for Communism and the Soviet occupation of Poland?"

59 Maurice Merleau-Ponty, *Humanism and Terror*, first published in French in 1947, another case in point of a brilliant philosopher's support of the reprehensible. The archetypical example is, of course, of Martin Heidegger and his relationship with Nazism.

60 I should be clear here that I recognize that there are other things that people who are called intellectuals do. They are experts and political operatives, for example.

61 See report of a University of Maryland study that shows ignorance about public issues is correlated with watching Fox News, www.businessinsider. com/extended-exposure-to-fox-news-may-be-detrimental-to-your-intelligence-2010–12#ixzz18aRyxPAt.

62 For a quick view of the range of opinion see Paul Krugman, "How Did Economists Get It So Wrong?" *New York Times*, September 2, 2009 and John H. Cochrane's response to this article, "How did Paul Krugman get it so Wrong?" http://faculty.chicagobooth.edu/john.cochrane/research/papers/krugman_response.htm.

References

Abu El-Haj, Nadia (2002), *Facts on the Ground: Archaeological Practice and Territorial Self Fashioning in Israeli Society*, Chicago: University of Chicago Press.

Al-Ju'beh, Nazmi (2003), "The Social Development of Jerusalem: A Society in Transition. The Impact of the Peace Process since Oslo Agreement 1993," unpublished manuscript.

Almond, Gabriel, and Sidney Verba (eds.) (1989), *Civic Culture*, Newbury Park: Sage.

Anderson, Perry (1976), *Considerations on Western Marxism*, London: Verso.

Andrzejewski, Jerzy (1997), *Ashes and Diamonds*, Chicago: Northwestern University Press.

Appiah, Kwame Anthony, and Henry Louis Gates Jr. (eds.) (2005), *Africana: The Encyclopedia of the African and African American Experience*, New York: Oxford University Press.

Arendt, Hannah (1958), *The Human Condition*, Chicago: University of Chicago Press.

—(1961), *Between Past and Future*, New York: Penguin Books.

—(1968), *The Origins of Totalitarianism*, New York: Harcourt.

Arjomand, Said (2008), *Constitutional Politics in the Middle East: With Special Reference to Turkey, Iraq, Iran and Afghanistan*, Oxford: Hart.

Armbruster, Ben (2008), "Krauthammer links Obama's Berlin speech to Hitler's Nazi Rallies," *Think Progress*, http://thinkprogress.org/2008/07/29/krautham-mer-obama-nazis/, accessed July 29, 2008.

Baker, Peter, and Helene Cooper (2009), "Obama Shifts Tone on Gates After Mulling Debate," *New York Times*, July 24, 2009, www.nytimes.com/2009/07/25/us/politics/25gates.html?_r=1&scp=18&sq=barack%20obama%20and%20henry%20louis%20gates&st=cse, accessed August 22, 2009.

—, Helene Cooper, and Adam Nagourney (2009), "Live Blogging Obama's News Conference," *New York Times*, July 22, 2009, http://thecaucus.blogs.nytimes.com

References

/2009/07/22/live-blogging-obamas-news-conference/?scp=2&sq=obama%20 on%20gates%20arrest,%20press%20conference,%20July%2022,%202009& st=cse, accessed August 20, 2009.

Baudrillard, Jean (1988), *Selected Writings*, Stanford: Stanford University Press.

Beck, Glenn (2009), "Is massive Health Care plan reparations?", http://www. glennbeck.com/content/articles/article/198/28317/, accessed August 17, 2009.

Bell, Daniel (1960), *The End of Ideology*, Cambridge, MA: Harvard University Press.

Bellah, Robert N., Richard Madsen, William M. Sullivan, Ann Swidler, and Steven M. Tipton (1985), *Habits of the Heart: Individualism and Commitment in American Life*, Berkeley: University of California Press.

Bernhard, Michael, and Henryk Szlajfer (1995), *From the Polish Underground: Selections from Krytyka, 1978–1993*, University Park: Pennsylvania State University Press.

Bisharat, George (2003), "Origins of the Middle East Crisis: Who Caused the Palestinian Diaspora?" *The Electronic Intifada*, 3 December.

Black, Ian (2009), "A Devastating Defeat for Iran's Green Revolution," in *The Observer*, June 14, 2009, http://www.guardian.co.uk/world/2009/jun/14/ iran-tehran-election-results-riots.

Blit, Lucjan (1965), *The Eastern Pretender: Bolesław Piasecki, His Life and Times*, London: Hutchinson.

Borowski, Tadeusz (1992), *This Way for the Gas, Ladies and Gentlemen*, London: Penguin Books.

Breitbart, Andrew (2009), "Obama's Accidental Gift on Race," *Real Clear Politics*, July 27,www.realclearpolitics.com/articles/2009/07/27/obamas_acci- dental_gift_on_race_97637.html, accessed August 20, 2009.

Brooks, David (2008), "A Defining Moment," *New York Times*, March 4, www. nytimes.com/2008/03/04/opinion/04brooks.html.

Burchell, Graham, Colin Gordon, and Peter Miller (eds.) (1991), *The Foucault Effect: Studies in Governmentality*, Chicago: The University of Chicago Press.

Certeau, Michel de (1984), *The Practice of Everyday Life*, Berkeley: University of California Press.

Chafets, Zev (2010a), *Rush Limbaugh: An Army of One*, New York: Penguin.

—(2010b), "The Limbaugh Victory," *The New York Times*, May 19, www. nytimes.com / glogin?URI=http://www.nytimes.com / 2010 / 05 / 20 / opinion/ 20chafets.html&OQ=_rQ3D1Q26scpQ3D17Q26sqQ3DRushQ2520Limbaugh Q2520andQ2520GlennQ2520BeckQ2520ObamaQ26stQ3Dcse&OP=3f5499 42Q2F7,%29m7FQ3CYQ7CQ3FQ3CQ3CQ2AR7RVMV7VK7RV7Q3CerQ5 DrQ3CQ5D7RVYu0Q51%29Q2AQ7CQ22uQ2AQ3E3, accessed November 17, 2010.

Chan, Sewell (2007), "The Abner Louima Case, 10 Years Later," *New York Times*, August 9, http://cityroom.blogs.nytimes.com/2007/08/09/the- abner-louima-case-10–years-later/.

References

Chomsky, Noam (1989), *Necessary Illusions: Thought Control in Democratic Societies*, Boston: South End Press.

Clinton, Bill (1996), "Inaugural Address," http://clinton4.nara.gov/WH/New/other/sotu.html, accessed December 17, 2010.

Cohen, Roger (2010), "The Real Jew Debate," *New York Times,* December 10, 2010, www.nytimes.com/2010/12/10/opinion/10iht-edcohen.html?_r=1&hp, accessed January 15, 2011.

Conquest, Robert (1986), *The Harvest of Sorrow: Soviet Collectivization and the Terror-Famine*, Edmonton: University of Alberta Press in Association with the Canadian Institute of Ukrainian Studies & London, Century Hutchinson.

Cooper, Helene, and Abby Goodnough (2009), "Over Beers, No Apologies, but Plans to Have Lunch," *New York Times*, July 31, www.nytimes.com/2009/07/31/us/politics/31obama.html?_r=1&scp=1&sq=Over%20Beers,%20No%20Apologies,%20but%20Plans%20to%20Have%20Lunch&st=cse.

D'Souza, Dinesh (2010) "How Obama Thinks," *Forbes.com*, www.forbes.com/forbes/2010/0927/politics-socialism-capitalism-private-enterprises-obama-business-problem.html, accessed January 15, 2011.

Dayan, Daniel, and Elihu Katz (1992), *Media Events: The Live Broadcasting of History*, Cambridge, MA: Harvard University Press.

Debord, Guy (1994), *The Society of the Spectacle*, New York: Zone Books.

Dewey, John (1991), *The Public and its Problems,* Athens, OH: Swallow Press.

Dionne, E.J. (2009), "The Real Town Hall Story," *The Washington Post,* September 3, www.washingtonpost.com/wp-dyn/content/article/2009/09/02/AR2009090202858.html.

Eliasoph, Nina (1998), *Avoiding Politics: How Americans Produce Apathy in Everyday Life*, Cambridge: Cambridge University Press.

—, and Paul Lichterman (2003), "Culture in Interaction," *American Journal of Sociology,* 108, 4: 735–94.

Esteron, Yoel (2003), "Who's in Favor of Annihilating Israel?" *Haaretz*, www.haaretz.com/print-edition/opinion/who-s-in-favor-of-annihilating-israel-1.107140, accessed January 15, 2011.

Eyal, Gil (2008), *The Disenchantment of the Orient: Expertise in Arab Affairs and the Israeli State*, Palo Alto: Stanford University Press.

Feher, Ferenc (1979), "Kadarism as the Model State of Krushchevism," in *Telos*, 40.

Fine, Gary Alan (1979), "Small Groups and Culture Creation: The Idioculture of Little League Baseball Teams," *American Sociological Review*, 44: 733–45.

—(1989), "Mobilizing Fun: Provisioning Resources in Leisure Worlds," *Sport Sociology Journal*, 6: 319–34.

—(1991), "On the Macrofoundations of Microsociology: Constraint and the Exterior Reality of Structure," *Sociological Quarterly*, 32: 161–77.

References

—(1998), *Morel Tales: The Culture of Mushrooming*, Cambridge, MA: Harvard University Press.

—(2000), "Games and Truth: Learning to Construct Social Problems in High School Debate," *Socio-logical Quarterly*, 41: 103–23.

—, and Brooke Harrington (2004), "Tiny Publics: Small Groups and Civil Society," *Sociological Theory*, 22, 3: 341–56.

—, and Lori Holyfield (1996), "Secrecy, Trust, and Dangerous Leisure: Generating Group Cohesion in Voluntary Organizations," *Social Psychology Quarterly*, 59: 22–38.

—, and S. Kleinman (1979), "Rethinking Subculture: An Interactionist Approach," *American Journal of Sociology*, 85: 1–20.

—, and Randy Stoecker (1985), "Can the Circle Be Unbroken: Small Groups and Social Movements," *Advances in Group Process*, 2: 1–28.

—, Tim Hallett and Michael Sauder (2004), "Myth and Meaning of Bowling Alone," *Society*, 41, 6: 47–9.

Fish, Stanley (2009), "Henry Louis Gates: Déjà Vu All Over Again," *The New York Times*, July 24, http://fish.blogs.nytimes.com/2009/07/24/henry-louis-gates-deja-vu-all-over-again/?scp=4&sq=the%20arrest%20of%20henry%20louis%20gates%20jr.&st=cse.

Foucault, Michel (1973), *The Order of Things: Archaeology of the Human Sciences*, London: Vintage.

—(1979), *Discipline and Punish: The Birth of the Prison*, London: Vintage.

—(1984), "Truth and Power," in Rabinow, 1984.

Frank, Thomas (2008), "The GOP Loves the American Heartland to Death," *The Wall Street Journal*, http://online.wsj.com/article/SB122100226859616967.html?mod=hpp_us_inside_today, accessed May 3, 2010.

Gates Jr., Henry Louis (2007), *Finding Oprah's Roots, Finding Your Own*, New York: Crown.

—, and Evelyn Brooks Higginbotham, (eds.) (2008), *African American Biography*, New York: Oxford University Press.

Gazit, Nir (n.d.), "Social Agency, Spatial Practices and Power: The Micro-Foundations of Fragmented Sovereignty in the Occupied Territories," Department of Sociology and Anthropology, The Hebrew University, Jerusalem, unpublished manuscript.

Geertz, Clifford (1977), *The Interpretation of Cultures*, New York: Basic Books.

—(1983), "Common Sense as a Cultural System," in Clifford Geertz, *Local Knowledge: Further Essays in Interpretive Anthropology*, New York: Basic Books, pp. 73–93.

Gerstenfeld, Manfred (2007), "Anti-Israelism and Anti-Semitism: Common Characteristics and Motifs," *Jewish Political Studies Review*, 19:1–2, Spring, see www.spme.net/cgi-bin/articles.cgi?ID=2702, accessed, January 15, 2011.

Gerth, Hans, and C. Wright Mills (1958), *From Max Weber*, Oxford: Oxford University Press.

References

Goffman, Erving (1959), *The Presentation of Self in Everyday Life*, New York: Anchor.

—(1967), *Interaction Ritual*, New York: Anchor.

Goldfarb, Jeffrey C. (1980), *The Persistence of Freedom*, Boulder: Westview Press.

—(1983), *On Cultural Freedom*, Chicago: University of Chicago Press.

—*(1989)*, *Beyond Glasnost: The Post-Totalitarian Mind*, Chicago: University of Chicago Press.

—(1991), *The Cynical Society: The Culture of Politics and The Politics of Culture in American Life*, Chicago: University of Chicago Press,

—(1992), *After the Fall: The Pursuit of Democracy in Central Europe*, New York: Basic Books.

—(1998), *Civility and Subversion: The Intellectual in Democratic Society*, Cambridge: Cambridge University Press.

—(2005), "Dialogue, Culture, Critique: The Sociology of Culture and the New Sociological Imagination," *The International Journal of Politics, Culture and Society*, June.

—(2006), *The Politics of Small Things: The Power of the Powerless in Dark Times*, Chicago: University of Chicago Press.

Goodnough, Abby (2009), "Harvard Professor Jailed; Officer Is Accused of Bias," *New York Times*, www.nytimes.com/2009/07/21/us/21gates.html.

Gouldner, Alvin (1980), *The Coming Crisis in Western Sociology*, New York: Basic Books.

Gramsci, Antonio (1971), *Selections from the Prison Notebooks*, New York: International Publishers Co.

Gross, Jan Tomasz (2001), *Neighbors: The Destruction of the Jewish Community in Jedwabne, Poland*, Princeton: Princeton University Press.

Grossman, David (1988), *The Yellow Wind*, New York: Farrar, Straus, and Giroux.

—(1993), *Sleeping on a Wire: Conversations with Palestinians in Israel*, New York: Farrar, Straus, and Giroux.

—(2004), "Letter to a Palestinian Friend," in Grossman, *Death as a Way of Life: Israel Ten Years after Oslo*, trans. Haim Watzam, New York: Picador.

—(2006), "Uri my son," accessed at www.voiceseducation.org/category/tag/evening-iwth-david-grossman-video, June 13, 2010.

Grotowski, Jerzy (2002), *Towards a Poor Theatre*, New York: Routledge.

Gutman, Yifat, and Jeffrey C. Goldfarb (2010), "The Cultural Constitution of Publics," in Grindstaff, John R. Hall, and Laura Ming-cheng Lo (eds.), *Handbook of Cultural Sociology*, London/New York: Routledge, pp. 495–503.

Hammami, Rema (2005), "On the Importance of Thugs: The Moral Economy of a Checkpoint," *Jerusalem Quarterly* (22/23), www.jerusalemquarterly.org/ViewArticle.aspx?id=109.

References

Havel Vaclav, et al., John Keane, ed. (1985), *The Power of the Powerless: Citizens Against the State in Central-Eastern Europe*, Armonk, NY: M. E. Sharpe Inc.

Herbert, Bob (2009), "Anger Has Its Place," *New York Times,* July 31, www.nytimes.com/2009/08/01/opinion/01herbert.html, accessed August 20, 2009.

Herszenhorn, David (2010), "Congress Now Has a 'Tea Party Caucus'," *The New York Times,* July 21, http://thecaucus.blogs.nytimes.com/2010/07/20/congress-now-has-a-tea-party-caucus/.

Hofstadter, Richard (1963), *Anti-intellectualism in American Life*, New York: Vintage Books.

Hollander, Paul (2006), *The End of Commitment: Intellectuals, Revolutionaries, and Political Morality*, Chicago: Ivan R. Dee.

Horkheimer, Max, and Theodor Adorno (2007), *The Dialectic of Enlightenment*, Palo Alto: Stanford University Press.

Hrabal, Bohumil (1990a), *I Served the King of England*, New York: Vintage International.

—(1990b), *Too Loud a Solitude*, San Diego: Harcourt.

Huntington, Samuel (1993), "The Clash of Civilizations?" *Foreign Affairs*, Summer 1993.

Jamieson, Kathleen Hall (1988), *Eloquence in an Electronic Age: The Transformation of Political Speech Making*, Oxford: Oxford University Press.

Janowitz, Morris (1971), *The Professional Soldier: A Social and Political Portrait*, New York: Free Press.

—,and James Burk (1991), *On Social Organization and Social Control*, Chicago: University of Chicago Press.

Jones, Angela (2009), *The Niagara Movement 1905–1910: Social Change and the Making of Black Publics*, dissertation, New School for Social Research.

Joravsky, David (1986), *The Lysenko Affair*, Chicago: University of Chicago Press.

Judt, Tony (2003), "Israel: The Alternative," *New York Review of Books*, October 23, www.nybooks.com/articles/archives/2003/oct/23/israel-the-alternative/, accessed January 15, 2011.

—(2006), *Postwar: A History of Europe since 1945*, London: Penguin Press.

Kakutani, Michiko (2010), "The Engine of Right-Wing Rage, Fueled by More Than Just Anger," *New York Times, Art Section,* September 14, http://query.nytimes.com/gst/fullpage.html?res=9E05E6D8143BF937A2575AC0A9669D8B63&scp=16&sq=Rush%20Limbaugh%20and%20Glenn%20Beck%20Obama&st=cse, accessed November 17, 2010.

Katznelson, Ira (2006), *When Affirmative Action was White: An Untold History of Racial Inequality in Twentieth-Century America*, New York: W.W. Norton and Company.

Khalidi, Rashid (2007), *The Iron Cage: The Story of the Palestinian Struggle for Statehood*, Boston: Beacon.

References

Khoury, Jack, and Barak Ravid (2010), "Lieberman: Talks Must Tackle Israeli Arabs' Citizenship," *Haaretz Daily Newspaper*, www.haaretz.com/print-edition/news/lieberman-talks-must-tackle-israeli-arabs-citizenship-1.314672, accessed January 13, 2011.

Khrushchev, Nikita (1956), www.marxists.org/archive/khrushchev/1956/02/24. htm, accessed July 8, 2009.

Kis, Danilo (1990), *Hourglass*, London: Faber.

Kitliński, Tomek, and Pawel Leszkowicz (n.d.), "A Letter from Poland: The Same Europe, the Other Hate?", LoveDifference, Europe and Intercultural Dialogue, http://lovedifference.wordpress.com/articlespodcasts/a-letter-from-poland-the-same-europe-the-other-hate/, accessed January 15, 2011.

Kołakowski, Leszek (1978), *Main Currents of Marxism*, Oxford: Oxford University Press.

Konrad, George (1974), *The Case Worker*, New York: Harcourt.

Konwicki, Tadeusz (1982), *The Polish Complex*, New York: Farrar Straus and Giroux.

—(1983), *A Minor Apocalypse*, New York: Farrar Straus and Giroux.

Kos (2009), "Birthers are mostly Republican and Southern," *Daily Kos*, www.dailykos.com/storyonly/2009/7/31/760087/-Birthers-are-mostly-Republican-and-Southern, accessed August 10, 2009.

Krabel, Ron (2002), *Starring Mandela and Cosby: Television, Identity, and the End of Apartheid*, Ph.D. dissertation, New School for Social Research.

Kumiega, Jennifer (1987), *The Theatre of Grotowski*, London: Methuen.

Kundera, Milan (1980), *The Book of Laughter and Forgetting*, New York: Alfred A. Knopf.

—(1984), *The Unbearable Lightness of Being*, New York: Harper and Row.

Kunicki, Mikołaj (2005), "The Red and the Brown: Bolesław Piasecki the Polish Communist and Anti-Zionist Campaign in Poland, 1967–68," *East European Politics and Societies*, 8, 2: 185–225.

Kuroń, Jacek, and Karol Modzelewski (1968), *A Revolutionary Socialist Manifesto: An Open Letter to the Party*, London: An International Socialism Publication.

Kuzio, Taras (ed.) (2007), *Aspects of the Orange Revolution VI: Post-Communist Democratic Revolutions in Comparative Perspective*, Stuttgart: *ibidem*-Verlag.

Leibovich, Mark (2008), "Palin Visits a 'Pro-America' Kind of Town," *New York Times*, October 17.

Lenin, Vladimir (1905), "Party Organization and Party Literature," originally published in *Novaya Zhizn*, 12, November 13, 1905. Source: Marxist Internet archive, http://marxists.catbull.com/archive/lenin/works/1905/nov/13.htm.

Levine, Donald (ed.) (1972), *Georg Simmel on Individuality and Social Forms*, Chicago: University of Chicago Press.

Lévy, Bernard-Henry (2007), *American Vertigo: Traveling America in the Footsteps of Tocqueville*, New York: Random House.

References

Lewis, Bernard (1990), "The Roots of Muslim Rage," *The Atlantic Monthly,* September, www.cis.org.au/Policy/summer01–02/polsumm01–3.pdf, accessed January 25, 2010.

Lewis, Flora (1958), *A Case History of Hope: The Story of Poland's Peaceful Revolutions,* New York: Doubleday.

Lichterman, Paul (1996), *The Search for Political Community: American Activists Reinventing Commitment,* New York: Cambridge University Press.

Lipset, S. Martin (1990), "The Centrality of Political Culture," *Journal of Democracy,* 1 1: 80–3.

Lipski, Jan Józef, Gene M. Moore, and Olga Amsterdamska (1985), *KOR: A History of the Workers' Defense Committee in Poland, 1976 – 1981,* Berkeley: University of California Press.

Luce, Edward, and Alexandra Ulmer (2009),"Obama Foes turn to '60s Radical for Tactical Tips," *Financial Times,* August 17, reprinted on *Freedom Works* website: www.freedomworks.org/news/obama-foes-turn-to-%E2%80%9960s-radical-for-tactical-tips.

Lukacs, Georg (1971), *Solzhenitsyn,* Boston: MIT Press.

McKinley Jr., James C. (2010), "Texas Conservatives Win Curriculum Change," *New York Times,* March 12, www.nytimes.com/2010/03/13/education/13texas.html, accessed January 15, 2011.

Marcuse, Herbert (1964), *One Dimensional Man,* New York: Beacon.

Marx, Karl, and Friedrich Engels (1998), *The German Ideology,* New York: Prometheus Books.

Matynia, Elżbieta (ed.) (1996), *Grappling with Democracy: Deliberations on Post-Communist Societies (1990–1995),* Prague: Sociologické Nakladatelství.

—(2001), "Furnishing Democracy at the End of the Century: Negotiating Transition at the Polish Round Table & Others," *Eastern European Politics and Society,* 15, 2: 454–71.

Mead, George Herbert (1963), *Mind, Self and Society,* Chicago: University of Chicago Press.

Merleau-Ponty, Maurice (1969), *Humanism and Terror,* Boston: Beacon Press.

Meyrowitz, Joshua (1986), *No Sense of Place,* Oxford: Oxford University Press.

Michlic, Joanna B., and Antony Polonsky (2004), *Neighbors Respond: The Controversy over the Jedwabne Massacre in Poland,* Princeton: Princeton University Press.

Michnik, Adam (1987), "A New Evolutionism," in *Letters from Prison and Other Essays,* Berkeley: University of California Press, pp.135–48.

—(1993), *The Church and the Left,* Chicago: University of Chicago Press.

Miłosz, Czesław (1955), *The Captive Mind,* New York: Vintage Books.

Mokrzycki, Edmund (1996), "Is the Intelligentsia Still Needed in Poland?",

References

International Conference Democratic Transitions in Latin America and in Eastern Europe: Rupture and Continuity, www.nevusp.org/downloads/seminarios/france96/2–2–Edmu.pdf.

Morley, Jefferson (2005), "The Branding of Lebanon's 'Revolution'," *Washington Post*, March 3, www.washingtonpost.com/wp-dyn/articles/A1911–2005Mar2.html.

Murray, Shailagh (2008), "Obama's Reagan Comparison Sparks Debate," *Washington Post*, http://voices.washingtonpost.com/the-trail/2008/01/17/obamas_reagan_comparison_spark_1.html, accessed August 19, 2008.

Myrdal, Gunnar (1944), *An American Dilemma: The Negro Problem and Modern Democracy*, New York: Harper & Bros.

New York Times (2009), "The Gates Case and Racial Profiling," *New York Times*, July 22, http://roomfordebate.blogs.nytimes.com/2009/07/22/the-gates-case-and-racial-profiling/?scp=13&sq=henry%20louis%20gates%20jr&st=cse, accessed August 20, 2009.

Newman, Maria (2009), "Varied Opinions on Gates Controversy Light Up the Web," *New York Times*, July 24, www.nytimes.com/2009/07/25/us/politics/25gatesblogs.html?scp=29&sq=henry%20louis%20gates%20jr.&st=cse, accessed August 21, 2009.

O'Donnell, Guillermo, et al. (eds.) (1986), *Transitions From Authoritarian Rule: Prospects for Democracy*, Baltimore: Johns Hopkins University Press.

Obama, Barack (2004), *Dreams from My Father: A Story of Race and Inheritance*, New York: Crown Publishers.

—(2006), *The Audacity of Hope: Thoughts on Reclaiming the American Dream*, New York: Crown Publishers.

—(2008), "The American Promise," Democratic Convention at INVESCO Field, Denver, Colorado, August 28, www.realclearpolitics.com/articles/2008/08/the_american_promise.html, accessed August 29, 2008.

On the Hill (2009), "Stunning 91% of Conservatives Call Obama 'Socialist,' 'Marxist,' 'Communist' Or 'Fascist'," May 21, http://onthehillblog.blogspot.com/2009/05/stunning-91–of-conservatives-call-obama.html, accessed August 10, 2009.

Page, Clarence (2009), "A Race Card From the Right Wing," *Chicago Tribune*, www.chicagotribune.com/news/columnists/chi-oped0816pageaug16,0,7822008.column, accessed August 17, 2009.

Palin, Sarah (2008), "Speech at the Republican National Convention in St. Paul," as provided by CQ Transcriptions, see http://elections.nytimes.com/2008/president/conventions/videos/transcripts/20080903_PALIN_SPEECH, accessed August 15, 2009.

Parker, Kate (2009), "Face the Nation or Meet the Press," www.youtube.com/watch?v=QeZnoJdq4rE, accessed January 15, 2011.

Parsons, Talcott (1971), *The System of Modern Societies*, Englewood Cliffs, NJ: Prentice Hall.

References

Paterson, Orlando (1985), *Slavery and Social Death: A Comparative Study*, Cambridge, MA: Harvard University Press.

Peeva, Ralitsa (2000), *The Bulgarian Round Table in Comparative Perspective* Ph.D. dissertation, New School for Social Research.

Pew Research Center for the People and the Press (2009), "Muslims Widely Seen As Facing Discrimination," http://people-press.org/report/542/muslims-widely-seen-as-facing-discrimination, accessed September 9, 2009.

Polish State Archives (1980), www.archiwa.gov.pl/memory/sub_listakrajowa/index.php?va_lang=en&fileid=022, accessed July 7, 2009.

Pollack, Harriet, and Christopher Metress (eds.) (2008), *Emmett Till in Literary Memory and Imagination*, Baton Rouge: Louisiana State University Press.

Postman, Neil (1986), *Amusing Ourselves to Death: Public Discourse in the Age of Show Business*, New York: Penguin Books.

Putnam, Robert D. (1995), "Bowling Alone: America's Declining Social Capital," *Journal of Democracy*, January: 65–78.

—(1996), "The Strange Disappearance of Civic America," *American Prospect*, 24, Winter: 34–48.

—(2000), *Bowling Alone: The Collapse and Revival of American Community*, New York: Simon & Schuster.

Pye, Lucian W. (1972), "Culture and Political Science: Problems in the Evaluation of the Concept of Political Culture," *Social Science Quarterly*, 53: 2, Sept.: 285–96.

—, and Sidney Verba (eds.) (1965), *Political Culture and Political Development*, Princeton: Princeton University Press.

Rabinow, Paul (ed.) (1984), *The Foucault Reader*, New York: Pantheon Books.

Reagan, Ronald (1981), "Inaugural Address," January 20, 1981, www.reaganlibrary.com/reagan/speeches/first.asp, accessed August 19, 2008.

Reeves, Richard (1982), *American Journey: Traveling with Tocqueville in Search of Democracy in America*, New York: Simon and Schuster.

Richards, Thomas (1995), *At Work with Grotowski on Physical Actions*, London: Routledge.

Rutenberg, Jim, and Jackie Calmes (2008), "False 'Death Panel' Rumor Has Some Familiar Roots," *New York Times*, August 13, www.nytimes.com/2009/08/14/health/policy/14panel.html, accessed January 15, 2011.

Sachs, Jeffrey (2005), *The End of Poverty: Economic Possibilities for Our Time*, New York: Penguin.

Sack, Kevin (2009), "Calm, but Moved to Be Heard on Health Care," *New York Times*, August 24, www.nytimes.com/2009/08/25/health/policy/25georgia.html?ref=politics, accessed August 26, 2009.

Said, Edward (1994), *Representations of the Intellectual: The 1993 Reith Lectures*, New York: Pantheon Books.

—(1999), "Truth and Reconciliation," *Al-Ahram Weekly* On-line, January

References

14–20, issue no. 412, http://weekly.ahram.org.eg/1999/412/op2.htm, accessed January 12, 2010.

—(2002), "Emerging Alternatives in Palestine," ZNET, January 15, www.zcom-munications.org/give-us-back-our-democracy-by-edward-said, accessed June 11, 2010.

—(2005), "The Only Alternative," in Edward Said, *From Oslo to Iraq and the Road Map*, New York: Vintage Books.

—(2007), "The Clash of Ignorance," *The Nation,* www.thenation.com/docprint. mhtml?i=20011022&s=said, accessed, January 25, 2010.

Scheppele, Kim Lane (2005), "Democracy by Judiciary," in Adam W. Czarnota et al. (eds.), *Rethinking the Rule of Law After Communism*, Budapest/New York: Central European University Press, pp. 25–60.

Schudson, Michael (1989a), "How Culture Works: Perspectives from Media Studies on the Efficacy of Symbols," *Theory and Society*, 18: 153–80.

—(1989b), *The Good Citizen*. New York: Free Press.

Schuetz, Janice E., and Lin S. Lilly (eds.) (1999), *The O. J. Simpson Trials: Rhetoric, Media and the Law*, Carbondale, IL: Southern Illinois University Press.

Shehadeh, Raja (2002), *Stranger in the House: Coming of Age in Occupied Palestine*, New York: Penguin.

Shulman, David (2007), *Dark Hope: Working for Peace in Israel and Palestine*, Chicago: University of Chicago Press.

Shulman, George (2008), *American Prophecy: Race and Redemption in American Political Culture*, Minneapolis: University of Minnesota Press.

Simmel, Georg (1972), "The Stranger," in Donald Levine (ed.), *Georg Simmel on Individuality and Social Forms*, Chicago: University of Chicago Press, pp. 143–9.

Simon Wiesenthal Center (2009), "The Cambridge Confrontation – Sgt Crowley and Professor Gates: An Open Invitation to the Real 'Teachable Moment'," www.wiesenthal.com/site/apps/nlnet/content2.aspx?c=lsKWLbPJLnF&b=444 1467&ct=7265017.

Slackman, Michael (2006), "30 Are Killed in Sinai as Bombs Rock Egyptian Resort City," *New York Times*, April 25, www.nytimes.com/2006/04/25/world/middleeast/25egypt.html.

Solzhenitsyn, Alexander (1963), *One Day in the Life of Ivan Denisovich*, New York: E. P. Dutton & Co.

Stein, Sam (2009), "Steele Calls Obama Health Care Socialism, Agrees This His Waterloo," *Huffington Post*, www.huffingtonpost.com/2009/07/20/steele-calls-obama-health_n_240989.html, accessed August 10, 2009.

Thomas, W. I. (1923), *The Unadjusted Girl*, New York: Little Brown.

Tismaneanu, Vladimir (2003), *Stalinism for All Seasons: A Political History of Romanian Communism*, Berkeley: University of California Press.

References

Tocqueville, Alexis de (2000), *Democracy in America*, Chicago: University of Chicago Press.

Urbina, Ian, and Katharine Q. Seelye (2009), "Senator Goes Face to Face With Dissent," *New York Times*, August 12, www.nytimes.com/2009/08/12/health/policy/12townhall.html?_r=1&hpw=&pagewanted=print.

US Department of Justice (2009), www.justice.gov/ag/speeches/2009/ag-speech-090218.html, accessed January 13, 2011.

Vajda, Mihaly (1979), "Is Kadarism an Alternative?" in *Telos*, 39, Spring: 172–9.

Verba, Sidney, and Norman H. Nie (1972), *Political Participation in America: Political Democracy and Social Equality*, New York: Harper and Row.

Wagner-Pacifici, Robin (2010), "The Restlessness of Events," *American Journal of Sociology*, 115, 5: 1351–86.

Washington Post (2004), www.washingtonpost.com/wp-dyn/articles/A19751–2004Jul27.html, accessed November 7, 2010.

Weber, Max (1978), *Economy and Society*, Berkeley: University of California Press.

West, Cornell (1989), *The American Evasion of Philosophy: A Genealogy of Pragmatism*, Madison: University of Wisconsin Press.

Wilentz, Sean (2008), *Age of Reagan: A History, 1974–2008*, New York: HarperCollins Publishers.

Wills, Garry (2008), "Two Speeches on Race," *New York Review of Books*, May, www.nybooks.com/articles/archives/2008/may/01/two-speeches-on-race/.

Wilson, William J. (1971), *The Declining Significance of Race: Blacks and Changing American Institutions*, Chicago: University of Chicago Press.

—(2001), *The Bridge over the Racial Divide: Rising Inequality and Racial Politics*, Berkeley: University of California Press.

Wong, Kristina (2009), "Poll: Obama's Popularity lifts US Global Image," *ABC News*, http://abcnews.go.com/Politics/story?id=8155223&page=1.

Zeleny, Jeff (2009), "Grassley Reassures Republican Constituents," *New York Times*, August 12, http://thecaucus.blogs.nytimes.com/2009/08/12/grassley-reassures-republican-constituents/, accessed September 3, 2009.

Zernike, Kate, and Megan Thee-Brenan (2010), "Poll Finds Tea Party Backers Wealthier and More Educated," *New York Times*, www.nytimes.com/2010/04/15/us/politics/15poll.html.

Index

Index

Index

Dean, Howard 93, 95, 106, 140
DeMint, Jim 92
democracy
  and American political culture 72,
    75, 79, 83, 88–92, 93–4
  and capitalism 24, 68, 75, 88–92
  and political culture 15–22
  and social science 22–5
  see also Tocqueville, Alexis de
Democracy Seminar (Poland) 65–7,
  68
democratic culture 135, 149, 150–74
  and intellectuals 158–74
Descarte, René 16, 17, 72
Dewey, John: *The Public and its
  Problems* 17
Dewind, Adrian 66
disciplinary power, in Israel–Palestine
  114–16, 118
Doric, Carolyn 90
Dowie, Ted 8
Drake, Richie 83
Durkheim, Émile 20

Eastern Europe *see* Soviet bloc
  (former)
economic development, and
  democracy 24
egalitarianism
  and American political culture 72
  and democracy 15, 18, 19, 21
Eliasoph, Nina 28–9
Emerson, Ralph Waldo 21
Encounter Point (film) 11–12
Engels, Friedrich 42
English literature, and democracy
  21–2
equality, and democracy 17, 18, 20,
  22

Falk, Feliks 4
Fanton, Jonathan 66
Faulkner, William 22

feminism 27
films
  and American political culture
    74–5, 75–6
  in the Soviet bloc 56–8
Fine, Gary Alan 27, 29
Fitzgerald, Scott 22
Foucault, Michel 16, 39, 40, 67,
  137
  and disciplinary power 114, 116
  on political power 30–1, 32, 33
  and truth regimes 71–2, 114, 135
Fox News 91, 98, 103–4, 139
Frankfurt School 34–5
freedom
  cultural 35
  and democracy 18
"Freedom Works" movement 98–9

Gaston, Monique 8
Gates, Henry Louis, Jr. 79, 84–8
Gazit, Nir 115
Geertz, Clifford 33–4, 35, 166
genetics, Marxism and the ideology
  of 42, 43
Geneva Agreements, on
  Israel–Palestine 38–9, 129
geo-politics 89
  and the clash of civilizations 131–4
Georgia 70
The German Ideology (Marx and
  Engels) 42
Goffman, Erving 101, 114, 120
Gomulka, Wladyslaw 47
Gramsci, Antonio 161
Gross, Jan: *Neighbors* 155–6
Grossman, David 169, 170–2, 173
Grotowski, Jerzy 48

Habermas, J. 94
Hammami, Rema 113–14, 119,
  120–4, 126–7
Harrington, Brooke 27

Index

Index

Index

Index

Index